Matthias Kaiser

Paul Auster's "The New York Trilogy" as Postmodern Detective Fiction

Magisterarbeit
an der Albert-Ludwigs-Universität Freiburg
Philosophische Fakultäten
Institut für Nordamerikastudien
Januar 1999 Ausgabe

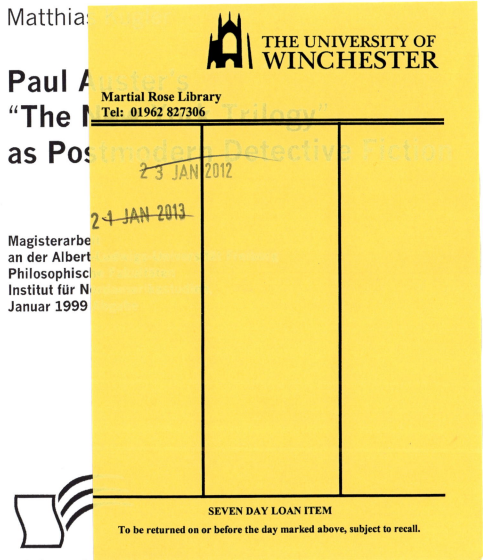

Diplomarbeiten Agentur
Dipl. Kfm. Dipl. Hdl. Björn Bedey
Dipl. Wi.-Ing. Martin Haschke
und Guido Meyer GbR

Hermannstal 119 k
22119 Hamburg

agentur@diplom.de
www.diplom.de

ID 1852

ID 1852
Kugler, Matthias: Paul Auster's "The New York Trilogy" as Postmodern Detective Fiction /
Matthias Kugler - Hamburg: Diplomarbeiten Agentur, 1999
Zugl.: Freiburg im Breisgau, Universität, Magister, 1999

Dipl. Kfm. Dipl. Hdl. Björn Bedey, Dipl. Wi.-Ing. Martin Haschke & Guido Meyer GbR
Diplomarbeiten Agentur, http://www.diplom.de, Hamburg
Printed in Germany

Diplomarbeiten Agentur

Wissensquellen gewinnbringend nutzen

Qualität, Praxisrelevanz und Aktualität zeichnen unsere Studien aus. Wir bieten Ihnen im Auftrag unserer Autorinnen und Autoren Wirtschafts- studien und wissenschaftliche Abschlussarbeiten – Dissertationen, Diplomarbeiten, Magisterarbeiten, Staatsexamensarbeiten und Studien- arbeiten zum Kauf. Sie wurden an deutschen Universitäten, Fachhoch- schulen, Akademien oder vergleichbaren Institutionen der Europäischen Union geschrieben. Der Notendurchschnitt liegt bei 1,5.

Wettbewerbsvorteile verschaffen – Vergleichen Sie den Preis unserer Studien mit den Honoraren externer Berater. Um dieses Wissen selbst zusammenzutragen, müssten Sie viel Zeit und Geld aufbringen.

http://www.diplom.de bietet Ihnen unser vollständiges Lieferprogramm mit mehreren tausend Studien im Internet. Neben dem Online-Katalog und der Online-Suchmaschine für Ihre Recherche steht Ihnen auch eine Online-Bestellfunktion zur Verfügung. Inhaltliche Zusammenfassungen und Inhaltsverzeichnisse zu jeder Studie sind im Internet einsehbar.

Individueller Service – Gerne senden wir Ihnen auch unseren Papier- katalog zu. Bitte fordern Sie Ihr individuelles Exemplar bei uns an. Für Fragen, Anregungen und individuelle Anfragen stehen wir Ihnen gerne zur Verfügung. Wir freuen uns auf eine gute Zusammenarbeit

Ihr Team der *Diplomarbeiten* Agentur

Dipl. Kfm. Dipl. Hdl. Björn Bedey –
Dipl. Wi.-Ing. Martin Haschke ——
und Guido Meyer GbR ————

Hermannstal 119 k ————
22119 Hamburg ————

Fon: 040 / 655 99 20 ————
Fax: 040 / 655 99 222 ————

agentur@diplom.de ————
www.diplom.de ————

For Esther.

TABLE OF CONTENTS

There will be a new form.

--Paul Auster--

0 Introduction

Paul Auster's *New York Trilogy*, published in one volume for the first time in England in 1988 and in the U.S. in 1990[1] has been widely categorised as detective fiction among literary scholars and critics. There is, however, a striking diversity and lack of consensus regarding the classification of the trilogy within the existing genre forms of the detective novel. Among others, Auster's stories are described as: "meta-anti-detective-fiction;"[2] "mysteries about mysteries;"[3] a "strangely humorous working of the detective novel;"[4] "very soft-boiled;"[5] a "metamystery;"[6] "glassy little jigsaws;"[7] a "mixture between the detective story and the *nouveau roman*;"[8] a "metaphysical detective story;"[9] a "deconstruction of the detective novel;"[10] "anti-detective-fiction;"[11] "a late example of the anti-detective genre;"[12] and being related to 'hard-boiled' novels by authors like Hammett and Chandler."[13] Such a striking lack of agreement within the secondary literature has inspired me to write this paper. It

---

[1] Originally, the three short novels *City of Glass*, *Ghosts* and *The Locked Room* were published separately between 1985 and 1986. All subsequent references are to the 1990 edition (published in New York City by Penguin Books) of the novel and are incorporated parenthetically in the text. For convenience, the following title abbbreveations will be used in this paper: *The New York Trilogy* (NYT), *City of Glass* (CoG), *Ghosts* (G) and *The Locked Room* (TLR).

[2] Madeleine Sorapure, "The Detective and the Author" in: Dennis Barone (ed.), *Beyond the Red Notebook* (Philadelphia: University of Pennsylvania Press, 1995), p.72.

[3] Bruce Bawer, "Doubles and more Doubles", *The New Criterion* 7:8, 1989, p.67.

[4] Toby Olson, "Metaphysical Mystery Tour", *New York Times Book Review*, November 3, 1985.

[5] Marc Chénetier, "Paul Auster's Pseudonymous World" in: Dennis Barone (ed.), *Beyond the Red Notebook* (Philadelphia: University of Pennsylvania Press, 1995), p.35.

[6] Rebecca Goldstein, "The Man Shadowing Black is Blue", *New York Times Book Review*, June 29, 1986, p. 13.

[7] Stephen Schiff, "Inward Gaze of a Private Eye", *New York Times Book Review*, January 4, 1987, p. 27.

[8] Colin Greenland, "The Novelist Vanishes", *Times Literary Supplement*, December 11-17, 1987, p. 1375.

[9] Norma Rowen, "The Detective in Search of the Lost Tounge of Adam: Paul Auster's *City of Glass*", *Critique* 32:2, 1990, p. 224.

[10] William Lavender, "The Novel of Critical Engagement: Paul Auster's *City of Glass*", *Contemporary Literature*, 34:2, 1993, p. 219.

[11] Anne K. Holzapfel, *The New York Trilogy: Whodunit? Tracking the Structure of Paul Auster's Anti-Detective Novels*, (New York: Peter Lang, 1996), p. 9.

[12] Barry Lewis, "The Strange Case of Paul Auster", *Review of Contemporary Fiction* 14:1, 1994, p. 60.

[13] Carin Freywald, "How Philip Marlowe came to New York City: The Hard-Boiled American Crime Novels in Paul Auster's *The New York Trilogy*", in: Peter Freese and Michael Porsche, *Popular Culture in the United States* (Essen: Die Blaue Eule, 1994), p. 143.

does not, however, elaborate further on this diversity of viewpoints although they all seem to have a certain validity and underline the richness and diversity of Auster's detective trilogy; neither do I intend to coin a new term for Auster's detective fiction. I would rather place *The New York Trilogy* within a more general and open literary form, namely postmodern detective fiction. This classifies Paul Auster as an American writer who is part of the generation that immediately followed the 'classical literary movement' of American postmodernism' of the 60s and 70s. His writing demonstrates that he has been influenced by the revolutionary and innovative postmodern concepts, characterised by the notion of 'anything goes on a planet of multiplicity' as well as by French poststructuralism. He may, however, be distinguished from a 'traditional' postmodern writer[14] through a certain coherence in the narrative discourse, a neo-realistic approach and by showing a certain responsibility for social and moral aspects going beyond mere metafictional and subversive elements. Many of the ideas of postmodernism were formulated in theoretical literary texts of the 60s and 70s and based on formal experiments include the attempt of subverting the ability of language to refer truthfully to the world, and a radical turning away from coherent narrative discourse and plot. These ideas seem to have been internalized by the new generation of postmodern writers of the 80s to such a degree that the ideas themselves turn into objects of investigation and experiment.[15] Paul Auster seems to be on the right way of leaving the stony ground of "The Literature of Exhaustion", which according to John Barth only leads to "replenishment" if we creatively make use of 'what has been there before'. "It might be conceivable to rediscover validly the artifices of language and literature--such far-out notions as grammar, punctuation...even characterization! Even *plot!*--if one goes about it the right way, aware of what one's predecessors have been up to."[16]

---

[14] By coining such a term as 'traditional' in connection with Postmodernism (which seems to be a contradiction in itself) I do not attempt to participate in the ongoing discussion whether we have come to the end of Postmodernism or whether a postmodern writer of the 80s and 90s might be considered a member of the club of the postmodern movement of the 60s and 70s. This paper attempts to describe a new form of detective fiction that clearly defines itself through the postmodern tradition of the anti-detective novel--a term introduced by William Spanos and later taken up by Stefano Tani--but at the same time goes beyond this form and takes it a step further into the new 'literary case' of the 80s.

[15] Following this argument, Madeleine Sorapure's definition of Auster's trilogy as "meta-anti-detective-fiction" (see above) seems to be the most adequate in a narrow sense of defining the genre.

[16] John Barth, "The Literature of Exhaustion", in: *The Friday Book* (New York: Putnam's Sons, 1984), p. 68.

This paper asserts that Paul Auster's NYT can be adequately described as a particular form of postmodern detective fiction that may be defined, or rather 'redefined'[17], as a form which on the one hand still makes use of several well-known variations of the detective novel that have developed during the long tradition of the genre, such as the classical and the hard-boiled detective novel; but which, on the other hand are only applied by Auster to deviate from this course, subvert the existing elements and deliberately negate the fundamental purposes of the genre by introducing a great variety of postmodern aspects. In this, Auster follows the tradition of the anti-detective novels by such authors as Pynchon or Robbe-Grillet. He does, however, create a new form, that goes even beyond the familiar features of the anti-detective novel by adding a neo-realistic approach, that links the traditional features of the genre with the experimental, metafictional and ironic features of postmodernism.

Only in the recent years has there been a certain critical response to the prose work of Paul Auster, who has been publishing poetry, translations and essays since the beginning of the 70s. He has acquired a certain reputation in Europe (especially in France through his translations of Mallarmé and several other French avant-garde poets as well as his special interest in philosophy) as well as later in the U.S. The publication of the NYT has raised a lot of interest in the works of Paul Auster, which has helped me to strengthen my arguments by having a large amount of secondary literature at my disposal. As should be the case with every work dealing with literature in general, this paper maintains a close proximity to the primary texts by using relevant quotes where appropriate.

To support the arguments in this paper, chapter 1 analyses the history of detective fiction to clarify the formula and cultural background of the classical, 'hard-boiled', and anti-detective story, how its history evolved, and what it seems to be evolving into through the work of authors like Paul Auster. The structure and context of the classical, the 'hard-boiled', and the anti-detective novel, provide a general orientation and a basis to categorise the NYT within the genre. Apparent patterns and styles connect the old detective novel and the new and provide us with evidence demonstrating that all three varieties can be found in Auster's stories.

---

[17] Anne M. Holzapfel has already structurally examined the trilogy by applying the concept of the anti-detective novel (see above).

In chapter 2, this paper discusses elements which are generally agreed on by scholars and critics in the relevant secondary literature to adequately characterise postmodernism and which are at the same time part of Paul Auster's postmodern aesthetic in the NYT such as: fragmentation, indeterminacy, self-less-ness, hybridization, the decentered subject, the doubling of characters, the blurring or non-existing boundaries between the fictional and the 'real' world, and the question of text, author(ity), reading, writing, reader and writer.

The following chapters analyse in detail each of the three novels *City of Glass*, *Ghosts*, and *The Locked Room* in the scope of such concepts as 'truth and meaning' (ch. 3), 'the quest for identity' (ch. 4), 'concepts of reading and writing' (ch. 5), 'language' (ch. 6) and 'intertextuality' (ch. 7), always taking into consideration the arguments of the first two chapters.

The conclusion to this paper concisely summarises the main points from earlier chapters and tentatively investigates the possible reasons for the commercial success of the NYT and the question whether Auster has added some new dimensions to modern literature.

1 The Detective Novel and its Development--A Historical Survey

The popularity of Paul Auster's NYT is partly due to the mechanisms and the success of traditional crime and mystery stories which serve as a framework and enable him to reflect on issues more profound than just 'whodunit'. I consider that an examination of the several variations of the detective novel is essential to discover, elaborate on and clarify aspects of Auster's novels that make him a postmodern representative of the genre. We find in Auster's trilogy the well-known patterns from the stories of Poe and Doyle as well as from the American hard-boiled detective fiction. These patterns are, however, parodistically deconstructed in order to subvert their inherent positivistic *Weltanschauung* and thus create a new form of detective fiction. Auster stimulates and tantalises the reader by often not fulfilling common detective-novel expectations. This chapter will shed some light on the familiar features of the detective novel and its different categories that have developed since the middle of the last century.

> M. Dupin had from my boyhood
> been one of my heroes.
> --Sir Arthur Conan Doyle--

1.1 The Classical Detective Story

The development of the genre begins in April 1841 with the publication of Edgar Allan Poe's "The Murders in the Rue Morgue", followed shortly by "The Mystery of Marie Roget" (1842) and "The Purloined Letter" (1845), presenting the Frenchman Dupin as the detective. Some critics, however, trace the invention of the genre back as far as the biblical story of Daniel, the Oedipus myth or Egyptian tales. However, if Daniel invented the art of detection, he certainly did not invent the detective story. And who is actually willing to place Sophocles among the group of serious contenders for the invention of the genre? If we accept Stefano Tani's assertion that "a genre is a form aware of itself and of its own conventions"[18], then the only possible originator would be Poe who established the standards of the classical detective story. The ideas of Poe were subsequently used and extended by Sir Arthur Conan Doyle with his famous Sherlock Holmes stories. The genre reached its peak of popularity during the period between the end of the 19th century and World War II. The years between the two world wars have been called the "golden age of the detective story."[19] Although created by Poe in America, examples of this variety mainly came from Great Britain, represented by such authors as Agatha Christie, E.C. Bently, Margery Allingham, and Cecil Day Lewis.

The structure of the classical detective story is determined by clear-cut rules and an emphasis on rationality, logic and ratiocination that reflect the popular impulses of the time and prepare the ground for the reader's participation in the intellectual game. This notion is stressed by S.S. Van Dine who formulated twenty rules for writing detective stories in 1928.[20] Tani underlines this aspect by saying that "[Poe's] invention comes at the philosophically appropriate moment, corresponding to the nineteenth-century rise of the scientific and optimistic attitude of positivistic philosophy towards reality through the development of technology."[21] Since the end of World War II, other formulas that, according to Cawelti "include some elements of the mystery archetype, but also stories of adventure or melodrama--the hard-boiled detective story, the spy story, the police procedural tale, the gangster saga, and the Enforcer's caper--have become increasingly popular. (...) It seems clear that the classical formula is related to a distinctive historical period and reflects attitudes and interests that are no longer as widespread as they were."[22]

In "The Murders in the Rue Morgue" and "The Purloined Letter" Poe defined the formula of the classical detective story so sharply and effectively that, until the emergence of the hard-boiled story in America, successive detective story writers

---

[18] Stefano Tani, *The Doomed Detective, The Contribution of the Detective Novel to Postmodern American and Italian Fiction* (Carbondale: Southern Illinois University Press, 1984), p. 1.
[19] Tani, p. 9.
[20] S.S. Van Dine, "Twenty Rules for Writing Detective Stories", in: *The Art of the Mystery Story*, ed. Howard Haycraft (New York: Biblo and Tannen, 1976), p. 189.
[21] Tani, p. 11.
[22] John G. Cawelti, *Adventure, Mystery, and Romance: Formula Stories as Art and Popular Culture* (Chicago: University of Chicago Press, 1976), p. 80.

largely based their work on Poe's inventions. Poe's rules, as described by Cawelti, give a very clear picture of the story's situation, action, characters and setting.[23]

1. *Situation*. The story begins with an unsolved crime which for most of the story already lies in the past. As Tzevtan Todorov has pointed out in his essay "The Typology of Detective Fiction"[24], this placing of the major event in a concealed 'first story' which has taken place prior to most of the narrated action compels the 'second story' of the latter to be relatively static. Our attention is focused on the slow process of uncovering the perpetrator of this particular crime as the story moves towards the elucidation of its mystery. To start the process of detection and to arrive at a solution, the detective obviously needs to be confronted with a crime, which is also subject to certain conventions. Van Dine puts it rather straightforward: "There simply must be a corpse in a detective novel, and the deader the corpse the better. No lesser crime than murder will suffice."[25] Accidents, suicide or even a guilty detective are out of the question.[26] According to Cawelti, "the crime must be a major one with the potential for complex ramifications, but the victim cannot really be mourned or the possible complexities of the situation allowed to draw our attention away from the detective and his investigation."[27]

2. *Pattern of action*. Cawelti finds six main phases, concerning the action pattern in Poe's stories: (a) introduction of the detective; (b) crime and clues; (c) investigation; (d) announcement of the solution; (e) explanation of the solution; (f) denouement. Although the sequence of the pattern is sometimes modified and parts collapse into each other, it is difficult to imagine a classical detective story which greatly differs from Poe's scheme.

Frequently, a minor episode marks the beginning of the story, in which the detective's analytic skills are demonstratred as, for example, in "Rue Morgue". A second possibility of introducing the detective is deployed in "The Purloined Letter": The narrator is "enjoying the twofold luxury of meditation and a meerschaum in

[23] cf. Cawelti, pp. 80-98.
[24] cf. Tzevtan Todorov, "The Typology of Detective Fiction", in: *The Poetics of Prose* (Ithaca: Cornell University Press, 1977), pp. 42-52. (cf. chapter 5.6 for more information on Todorov's assertions and the question of plot in the NYT)
[25] Van Dine, p. 190. (Poe's story "The Purloined Letter" makes an exception here as the crime is associated with political intrigue).
[26] cf. Van Dine, p. 190.
[27] Cawelti, p. 81.

company with my friend C. Auguste Dupin, in his little back library (...)"[28], when the sudden intrusion of the Prefect G. from the outside world' breaks the placid calm. Conan Doyle elaborated this intrusion of the outside world into the memorable opening scenes at 221B Baker Street, where Holmes and Watson enjoy a similar reflective and contemplative atmosphere. The peaceful beginning in the detective's snug retreat establishes a point of departure and return for the story. The crime symbolises a disruption of the normal order of society and thus forces the detective to get actively involved in the case and give up his detached life for a limited time until order and harmony have been restored. Only "(...) when we arrive at the detective's solution, have [we] arrived at the truth, the single right perspective and ordering of events"[29], and only then may the detective return to his previous state of existence.

The description of the crime usually follows the introduction of the detective. Cawelti maintains that "the crime must be surrounded by a number of tangible clues that make it absolutely clear that some agency is responsible for it, and second, it must appear to be insoluble."[30]

The investigation, which immediately follows the "crime and clues" section, is constituted by the parade of suspects, witnesses, and false solutions, which further obfuscate the mystery, while seemingly moving toward the clarification of the case. As the reader gradually loses track of the case, his confusion mounts until he feels totally lost "in a murky and impenetrable bog of evidence and counterevidence."[31] Yet, by means of his rationality, his analytical skills and his intuition, the detective has solved the mystery and the case has been brought to a close.

The reader is rewarded for his efforts by the most crucial element of the detective story: the solution as explained by the detective himself. "The solution is (...) the final and fulfilling link in the detective novel's sequence, the one that gives sense to the genre and justifies its existence."[32] When the solution is announced, an important change in narrative perspective takes place. The typical anonymous narrator--generally described as 'Dr Watson figure' after the prominent character in

---

[28] Edgar Allan Poe, "The Purloined Letter", in: *The Fall of the House of Usher and other Writings*, ed. David Galloway (London: Penguin, 1986), p. 330.
[29] Cawelti, p. 89.
[30] Cawelti, p. 85.
[31] Cawelti, p. 86.
[32] Tani, p. 41.

Conan Doyle's story--is close to the detective but does not participate in his perceptions or process of reasoning. This enables the author to direct certain sympathies or antipathies at will and keeps the reader from prematurely solving the crime since the detective's companion is mostly unable to comprehend the detective's proceedings. The classical story's narrative method does not encourage an identification between the reader and the detective as the latter's feelings remain largely hidden. The reader rather identifies with the narrator figure or certain suspects (as e.g. Adolphe LeBon, quite a telling name). Upon reaching the explanation of the solution we suddenly encounter a shift to the detective's point of view.[33] The mystery that seemed to be so confusing and chaotic is revealed as clear and logical. The reader now joins the detective in his superior position. The explanation is important because "in completing the investigation it represents the goal toward which the story has been moving."[34]

The final section in the pattern of the classical detective story usually involves the confession and often also the arrest of the criminal. Although Poe distinctly separates solution and denouement in "Rue Morgue", they can also be combined. However, as Poe demonstrated in "The Purloined Letter", the actual representation of the denouement is not essential to the detective story. The final 'trap-scene' is only alluded to briefly as the reader may very well imagine its outcome. Moreover, the elaborate treatment necessary to present such a denouement would have completely taken the reader's attention away from Dupin and his success.

3. *Characters and relationships.* The classical detective story requires four main roles: (a) the victim; (b) the criminal; (c) the detective; and (d) those threatened by the crime but incapable of solving it.

Neither victim nor criminal are figures which are treated with much emotional interest or complexity. Although the criminal's actions may be interesting and his motives complex, they must primarily be evil and their deeds therefore always bad. The Minister D. or Professor Moriarty may be fascinating characters but they always have to be kept subordinated to the detective. Thus, the story's primary emphasis is placed on those who investigate the crime.

---

[33] "The Purloined Letter" is a good example to underline this particular aspect. Cf. Poe, pp. 345ff.
[34] Cawelti, p. 88.

The detective naturally gets the most attention in the story. His firm character, coherent personality, professional expertise and superior intellect distinguish him from the other characters present in the story. The detective is almost always a detached bachelor, an outsider. "There must be no love interest. The business on hand is to bring a criminal to the bar of justice, not to bring a lovelorn couple to the hymenal altar."[35] The detective keeps his distance from the case since too much emotional involvement could distract him from using his rational skills.[36]

The fourth main group of characters includes three main types: the offshoots of Poe's narrator, the members of the official police and, finally, the collection of false suspects. "[They] represent the norm of middle-class society suddenly disrupted by the abnormality of crime. The special drama of crime in the classical detective story lies in the way it threatens the serene domestic circles of bourgeois life with anarchy and chaos."[37] The attempts of the police to solve the case frequently turn out to be fruitless and their work proves to be ineffective as they lack the intuitive skills of the detective.

In a classical detective story, there is usually no room for the extensive description of any of the characters or of life in general that could distract the reader from following the case and sticking close to the detective. "If character means anything, we must admit that most of [the stories] have very little of it."[38]

> A detective novel should contain no long descriptive passages, no literary dallying with side-issues, no subtly worked-out character analyses, no 'atmospheric' preoccupations. (...) They hold up the action, and introduce issues irrelevant to the main purpose, which is to state a problem, analyse it, and bring it to a succesful conclusion.[39]

Anne M. Holzapfel, however, takes this point a little too far by claiming that "within the strictness of the Poesque detective novel there is no room for ambitious literary or philosophical reflection."[40] In my view, Poe's stories do emphasise certain

---

[35] Van Dine, p. 190f.

[36] For Poe's Dupin, however, money and personal revenge do influence his decisions to take on a case.

[37] Cawelti, p. 96.

[38] Michael Holquist, "Whodunit and Other Questions: Metaphysical Detective Stories in Postwar Fiction", in: Glenn W. Most and William W. Stowe (eds.), *The Poetics of Murder: Detective Fiction and Literary Theory* (San Diego: Harcourt, 1983), p. 158.

[39] Van Dine, p. 191f.

[40] Anne M. Holzapfel, *The New York Trilogy: Whodunit?*, p. 13

10

philosophical questions.[41] What is certainly true, however, is that there is a lack of trivial side issues in Poe's stories. The classical detective story focuses on matters of good and evil to "give the readers an opportunity to distance themselves from so-called high brow literature.[42] Especially in the changing times of the early 20th century many intellectuals were searching for a retreat from literature into the pleasure of leisurely reading. Michael Holquist states that during this particular time

> all the certainties of the 19th century--positivism, scientism, historicism--seem to have broken down. Dangerous questions are raised, the world is a threatening, unfamiliar place, inimical more often than not to reason. Is it not natural to assume, then, that often during this period when rationalism is experiencing some of its most damaging attacks, that intellectuals, who experienced these attacks first and most deeply, would turn for relief and easy reassurance to the detective story, the primary genre of popular literature which they, during the same period, were in fact, consuming? The same people who spent their days with Joyce were reading Agatha Christie at night.[43]

What the intellectual class needed was a form of escapism in which "the outside threat is resolved in an exorcising and entertaining ritual, consumed in two hours of escape from everyday cares in the 'den' of a comfortable house."[44]. Complex issues of modern life would require too much effort from the reader and are thus excluded. A more detailed examination of society's problems is reserved for the American hard-boiled novel and the anti-detective novel.

4. *Setting.* In devising the two isolated settings in "Rue Morgue" and "The Purloined Letter", Poe again set the standard pattern for the classical detective story. Dupin's apartment and the room in which the crime takes place are clearly marked off from the chaos of the outside world. This setting performs many functions: "First of all, it furnishes a limited and controlled backdrop against which the clues and suspects so central to the story can be silhouetted. It abstracts the story from the complexity and confusion of the larger social world and provides a rationale for avoiding the consideration of those more complex problems of social injustice and group conflict that form the basis of much contemporary realistic fiction."[45] Furthermore, the contrast between the outside world and the isolated room

---

[41] I refer the reader to Poe's elaborations on analysis, the distinction between the poet and the mathematician and the focus on imagination versus ratiocination among the great variety of aspects mentioned.
[42] Holzapfel, p. 13.
[43] Holquist, p.163f.
[44] Tani, p. 21.
[45] Cawelti, p. 97.

constitutes a symbolic representation of the relation between chaos and order, between rationality and confusion, between good and evil. As soon as a crime has disrupted the social order, the detective intervenes and by solving the case the chaos has been brought under control and order has been restored. This cyclic principle of the classical detective story is also reflected in the setting: The detective's apartment represents the starting and the end point of the detective's excursion to the outside world.

We could summarise that a conventional detective story is a fiction in which a detective, amateur or professional, tries to discover the solution of a mysterious case, generally a crime, usually a murder. The presence of at least five elements must therefore be made certain: the crime, the detective, the criminal, the process of detection, and the solution. With his Dupin stories, Edgar Allan Poe set the standard for the formula of the classical detective story. The elaboration of the Poesque ratiocinative tradition in Great Britain at the end of the 19th century and the success of Conan Doyle's Sherlock Holmes stories initiated its period of greatest popularity between the two World Wars. The United States experienced at around the same time an introduction of anti-Poesque innovation, which shall be dealt with in the next section.

> In my less stilted moments I also write
> detective novels.
> --Raymond Chandler--

1.2 The Hard-Boiled Detective Novel

Authors like Raymond Chandler and Dashiell Hammett created the so-called hard-boiled detective story that can be seen as a direct reaction to the Poesque type of story. The classical detective story was considered to be too artificial, too far away from reality and too 'British' for America. The detached 'super intellectual' detective of the Poesque tradition did not appeal to the new generation of mystery writers that published their crime fiction in 'pulp' magazines in the late 20s and 30s. A change in the form as well as in the content of the detective story better corresponded to an urban American culture that did not have anything in common with the idyllic countryside or London fog-bound street settings of the British detective novel. The 'heroic adventure' replaced the 'pure secret', changing the underlying archetype of the detective story.[46] The old issue of good over evil and rational over irrational was abolished, since the complexities of life, which were formerly excluded from the stories, now play as much a role as does the pursuing of the culprit or the solution of the case. "(...) Evil has become endemic and pervasive; it has begun to crumble the very pillars of middle-class society, respectable citizens, the modern metropolis, and the institutions of law and order."[47] Now, evil is a presupposed and existing part of society, and crime a daily phenomenon in the jungle of the American city.

In his famous essay "The Simple Art of Murder", Raymond Chandler concisely summarises the innovations in the genre referring to his 'colleague' Dashiell Hammett (who actually used to be a 'real' detective in his 'real' life):

> Hammett took murder out of the Venetian vase and put it back to the kind of people that commit it for reasons, not just to provide a corpse; and with the means at hand, not hand-wrought dueling pistols, curare and tropical fish. He put these people down on paper as they were, and he made them talk and think in a language they customarily used for these purposes.[48]

Among other aspects, Chandler stresses the notion of language, referring to the British English, which was so distinctly different from the vocabulary and style used by ordinary American people in such "man-made deserts"[49] as Los Angeles and New York. If we stick to the course set in the last chapter and concentrate on the five invariable elements that are inherent to the classical detective story, we find that a number of changes have taken place, concerning the process of detection, the detective and the solution.

The process of detection is no longer only the solution of a riddle but rather the quest for truth in a reality far more complex and ambigious than in the stereotyped structure of the classical British tradition.[50] According to Chandler, it is

---

[46] cf. Cawelti, p. 142.
[47] Cawelti, p.156.
[48] Raymond Chandler, "The Simple Art of Murder", in: Howard Haycraft (ed.), *The Art of the Mystery Story* (New York: Biblo and Tannen, 1976), p. 234.
[49] Cawelti, p. 155.
[50] cf. Tani, p. 23.

"this man's [i.e. the detective's] adventure in search of a hidden truth"[51] that motivates the new genre.

Now, the detective is a "hard-boiled dick, a lonely hero who clings to a personal code, no matter how absurd his devotion to it may seem."[52] He replaces Dupin and Sherlock Holmes and becomes a new anti-hero and a prototypical outsider in a corrupt society. In accordance with their strive for more realism, the American authors designed this character in such a way that he is not spared the adversities of life. He is a "tough guy" on the outside, showing a resistance towards physical harm, but is also a man of honor possessing moral values that are not initially obvious from the "tough guy's" appearance and behavior.

> (...) Down these mean streets a man must go who is not himself mean, who is neither tarnished nor afraid. The detective in this kind of story must be such a man. He is the hero, he is everything. He must be a complete man and a common man and yet an unusual man. He must be (...) a man of honor, by instinct, by inevitability. (...) He must be the best man in his world and a good enough man for any world. (...) He is a common man or he could not go among common people. (...) He is a lonely man and a proud man. (...) The story is his adventure in search of a hidden truth, and it would be no adventure if it did not happen to a man fit for adventure. (...) If there were enough like him, I think the world would be a very safe place to live in, and yet not too dull to be worth living in.[53]

This genre demythicises the detective, who is no longer a genius as Dupin and Holmes were, but is a normal man with a hangover the next morning. As Edward Margolies says, the hard-boiled detective's relentless and risky search for truth goes beyond mere job routine and implies a "moral, if not metaphysical quest."[54] Margolies further continues, "thus it may be that the ancestors of M. Dupin derive from the rationalists of the Enlightenment while the ancestors of the hard-boiled private eyes derive from those legendary medieval knights who most Americans first got to know via the novels of Scott and 19th century gothic romances."[55] A short example from Chandlers's *Farewell, My Lovely* will underline this argument:

> I got up on my feet and went over to the bowl in the corner and threw cold water on my face. After a little while I felt a little better, but very little. I needed a drink, I needed a

---

[51] Chandler, p. 237.
[52] Tani, p. 22.
[53] Chandler, p. 237.
[54] Edward Margolies, "The American Detective Thriller and the Idea of Society", in: Larry N. Landrum, Pat Browne, Ray B. Browne (eds.), *Dimensions of Detective Fiction* (Bowling Green, Ohio: Bowling Green University Popular Press, 1976), p. 84.
[55] ibid, p. 84.

vacation, I needed a home in the country. What I had was a coat, a hat and a gun. I put them on and went out of the room.[56]

The private eye is not aloof from the case, which is due to his moral obligations and to the more complex relations to the other characters in the novel. These relations could include, for example, a developing love affair with the female 'later-to-be-culprit'. Another possibility for his motivation to solve the case could be that he has a personal involvement--for example when a friend was the victim or when the detective has to prove his own innocence. The narrative perspective supports the personal interest of the detective in the quest in such a way that he himself is the narrator of the events. The reader empathises with him and is also closer to the action and capable of comprehending the events. However, this also makes the reader more vulnerable to fall into the same traps the detective has been lured into.

The genre of the classical detective story in which the qualities of the characters used to be only of peripheral importance, was substantially changed by the American hard-boiled story. The American writers of detective stories strove for characters that "were more fully rounded, (...) settings more ordinary, (...) plots less implausible and a detective [that] is more human"[57] to produce the appropriate atmosphere of 'reality'. From the classical formula, the hard-boiled novel takes the conventional setting of the detective's secure retreat and modifies it to suit its principles. The beginning of the story usually takes place in the shabby office of the private eye, in which he is visited by some peculiar and shady-looking figure, presenting him with a case that forces him into the outside world of evil, chaos and disorder. Since evil is inherent within society, the investigator is only able to restore a momentary order when the case is solved. The solution is therefore assigned a secondary role as for the detective the role of morals and honor seem to be more important than determining a flawless proof of the case against the criminal. This new notion of reality defies the neat solutions and the simple truths of the very logical and very artificial British detective novel. Cawelti adds that the detective has to surpass the crime's solution and is forced to come to a personal decision.[58] After having at least partially solved the case--the degree of success is an open variable that

---

[56] Raymond Chandler, *Farewell, My Lovely* (Harmondsworth: Penguin, 1975), p.206f.
[57] Holquist, p.163.
[58] cf. Cawelti, p.142.

15

differs from the perfect rate of success that we know from the rational 'super brain' of the Poesque tradition--the investigator returns to his office. The linearity of the plot and the circular structure are thus kept up, even though law and order are only temporarily restored. Finally, Raymond Chandler concisely summarises the differences between the hard-boiled story and the classical story by claiming that

> the cool-headed constructionist does not also come across with lively characters, sharp dialogue, a sense of pace and an acute use of observed detail. (...) The scientific sleuth has a nice new shiny laboratory but I'm sorry I can't remember the face. The fellow who can write you a vivid and colorful prose simply won't be bothered by the coolie labor of breaking down unbreakable alibis.[59]

Similarly, as American writers like Chandler, Hammett and others created a new form of detective fiction to adapt the traditional British form to a different world in America, postmodern writers tried to react after World War II to a radically changing development and perception of Western culture. Their playful deviation from the detective novel is the focus of attention in the next section.

Why is everybody so interested in texts?
--Thomas Pynchon--

1.3 The Anti-Detective Novel

William Spanos was the first to coin the term 'anti-detective novel'[60] in his essay "The Detective and The Boundary: Some Notes on the Postmodern Literary Imagination"[61], describing it as "the paradigmatic archetype of the postmodern literary imagination (...) the formal purpose of which is to evoke the impulse to

---

[59] Chandler, *The Simple Art of Murder*, p. 225.

[60] The other pioneer on this field is Michael Holquist who refers to the anti-detective novel as "metaphysical' detective novel in his remarkable essay "Whodunit and other Questions", which I have already dealt with further above. He quite generally maintains that postmodernism differs from modernism in its aesthetics; the latter showing psychological and mythical tendencies, whereas the former exactly denies these tendencies, thus creating a "kind of do-it-yourself detective story [that] has taken the place of myth as structuring principle in modernist literature." [Manfred Pütz, *The Story of Idenity: American Fiction of the Sixties*, (München: Wilhelm Fink, [2]1987), p.261.

[61] Originally published in *Boundary* 2:1, 1972, pp.147-68. repr. in: William V. Spanos, *Repetitions, The Postmodern Occasion in Literature and Culture* (Baton Rouge: Louisiana State University Press, 1987), pp. 13-49.

'detect' and/or to psychoanalyse in order to violently frustrate it by refusing to solve the crime (or find the cause of the neurosis)."[62] The nature of the anti-detective novel reflects the character of its time. Postmodernist writers such as Borges, Robbe-Grillet, Nabokov and Pynchon have made use of the detective story conventions and techniques with the precise intention of expressing the disorder and the existential void in our Western culture. Notions that are central to postmodernist theory, by means of a genre that was designed to epitomise the contrary. A fragmented world, political and cultural disorientation and insecurity and the bitter experience of World War II caused a radical shift in literature and other arts. The general loss of orientation was answered by new strategies. One approach was to exploit pre-existing forms of literature since, according to John Barth, one of the pioneers of the postmodern movement, literature as such has exhausted itself. He considered that the only salvation lay in our effort to ironically play with pre-existing forms. Classical detective fiction with its clear-cut structure suits this deviation perfectly. Tani asserts that "the conventions of the detective novel are more exploited than renewed by these writers, who deconstruct the genre's precise architecture into a meaningless mechanism without purpose: they parody positivistic detection."[63] The popular detective novel was accordingly lifted onto a higher and more literary level. Postmodernism's lack of a center, its refusal to posit a unifying system, its absence of a finality and therefore its nonexistent solution matches exactly the anti-detective novel.[64] Facts that were derived from the classical and hard-boiled novel, now become uncertain as the reader's expectations and hopes are often left unfulfilled, which results in disappointment and frustration. The detective's place as the central and ordering character of the novel is taken by the decentering and chaotic admission of mystery and nonsolution. The border between trivial literature and literary pretension are fluent and blend into one another. Parody, pastiche and intertextuality are frequently used stylistic devices and techniques of the new genre. Fragmentation, decenteredness, indeterminacy, absence, nonsolution and nothingness are predominant elements of the postmodern aesthetic and are motivated by the growing uncertainties of Western society and civilisation. Many postmodern writers

---

[62] Spanos, *Repetitions*, p. 46
[63] Tani, p. 34.
[64] cf. Holquist, p.170f.

discovered the detective genre as a perfect ground for their experiments and ironic playfulness.

The new form only works if the reader is first lulled into the safe familiarity of a conventional detective novel in the Poesque tradition. The detective, the crime, the other characters and the process of detection are all present and the linear movement of the plot seems to be under way. As the story proceeds, these elements are soon made out to be nonsense and are further complicated, turned upside down and ironically subverted. The detective's quest for a hidden truth seems to be similar to the hard-boiled form but often turns into a totally unfulfilled quest. The most crucial difference can therefore be made out in the treatment of the solution, which usually justifies the whole existence of the genre. It is often kept from the reader and familiar elements of the story do not form a whole, but remain separate entities without coherent meaning.[65] Conventions are paradoxically functional in the disintegration of the genre. Stefano Tani distinguishes three different techniques for handling the solution, or rather nonsolution, that also correspond to his categorisation of the anti-detective novel into three different groups: First, the 'innovative anti-detective novel', in which an early solution disappoints the reader and an unexpected final one totally puzzles him. A social preoccupation is predominant in these stories and partially resemble the hard-boiled school of the American tradition. Second, the 'deconstructive anti-detective novel', in which the solution is suspended and the novel frustratingly ends a few pages before the denouement. The detective is on an existential quest for truth in the world, or should we say *the* worlds? Third, the 'metafictional anti-detective novel', in which the detective genre is exploited to let the reader detect the hidden (written) text. It stresses the self-reflexivity of literature by questioning aspects that are natural within the context of the standard formula. The solution is hidden from the reader, who is desperately trying to make sense out of the relation between text, intertext, fact and fiction, the 'real' and the fictive world and the relation between author(ity) and character.[66] It has to be mentioned that none of these groups only refer to *a* particular novel, since overlappings are possible and always welcome and intended by the writers. Paul Austers NYT, for instance, seems to fit all three forms as we will find out later.

---

[65] cf. Tani, p. 41.
[66] cf. Tani, p. 43.

The detective no longer represents the order-establishing center of the story as the confusion he creates is greater than his detective talent. Rational thinking and a clear mind are blocked by his inner conflicts and his pointless quest for meaning. Early examples of the anti-detective novel by Borges or Robbe-Grillet comprise a labyrinth-like structure which emphasise the non-existent exit. Mirror images and doublings often go along with and support this confusing element.[67] Doublings are present in the form of doubled characters, allusions to other literary texts or repetitions of certain events of the plot. Porter discusses this function with regard to Borges' work, it could, however, also be applied to other anti-detective novels.

> Borges' researchers find themselves facing a spectral reality composed of an endlessly receding series of repetitions and reproductions. The manical pursuit of meaning and order conducted by his (...) detective goes on. The images beckon, but the patterns that form instantly dissolve. Thus, in the end, the investigator finds he is without the instruments required for distinguishing the mirror from the wall and with no vantage point from to comprehend the architecture of the whole.[68]

The detective is a humanist, an archeologist, a map-maker, a maker of meaning, trying to map the labyrinth of crime and thus find a solution that can be equalised with a map. The readers themselves cannot avoid repetitions, doublings, mirror images and labyrinths either. Like the detective, they have to learn to read the 'postmodern signs' on a different level. Therefore, the structure of the novel cannot be circular and coherent since the solution is missing and the readers are not returned to the secure state of order that existed before the crime had been committed. Dennis Porter states that "[in] place of the pleasure machine of popular fiction that returns its reader to the safety of his point of departure once the thrilling circuit of it is completed, many modern tales are machines without exits."[69] The anti-detective story is "nonteleological, is not concerned to have a neat ending in which all the questions are answered, (...) it is not a story, but a process."[70] As we will see, Paul Auster works with the aspects of the anti-detective novel but also stresses the importance of the 'story', that seems to have been neglected by the early postmodern movement.

---

[67] cf. Tani, p.47.
[68] Dennis Porter, *The Pursuit of Crime* (New Haven: Yale University Press, 1981), p. 246
[69] ibid, p. 246.
[70] Holquist, p.170f.

The anti-detective novel presents itself as a stable genre that can be seen as a continuation in the long development of the genre. This chapter has elaborated on a historical survey of the detective novel, on its elements, characteristic features, different forms and literary development, and has established the knowledge base to turn to the work of Paul Auster and examine his trilogy in the light of these developments. Yet prior to that step, the following chapter briefly introduces terms which are frequently ascribed to postmodernism by the relevant secondary literature. I will confine myself to those postmodern features which Auster incorporates in his texts and in doing so transforms a conventional detective story into postmodern detective fiction with its conception of experience as fractured, arbitrary, and incoherent.

> The ideal mystery is one you would read
> if the end was missing.
> --Raymond Chandler--

2 Postmodernism and Detective Fiction

2.1 Postmodernism and *The New York Trilogy*

Paul Auster' novels have their place in the postmodern tradition. In order to define the postmodern elements in the NYT, the most dominant features are briefly discussed with examples from Ihab Hassan's and Ulrich Broich's frameworks before they are applied to and verified in Auster's texts.

Ihab Hassan published a variety of essays[71] on the popular question among literary critics and scholars of how to define postmodernism. Instead of suggesting a definition, he offers a selective catena of terms of which the most fitting and appropriate ones regarding Auster's texts are:

1. *Indeterminacy*, which includes ambiguities, ruptures, and displacements affecting knowledge and society.[72]

2. *Fragmentation*, which is directly linked to indeterminacy or often follows from it. According to Hassan, the postmodernist's enemy number one is any sort of 'totalization'. All he pretends to trust are fragments. Typical postmodern preferences are hence collage, cut-up literary objects or montage.[73]

3. *Self-less-ness, Depth-less-ness*. Here, Hassan attains Nietzsche's theory that "the subject is only a fiction" which accounts for the 'loss of self' [which then results in the search for identity] in modern literature. The 'deep' Romantic ego is suppressed by postmodernism and loses itself in the game of language [a predominat feature in the NYT as we will see], in the differences from which reality is plurally made and in its impersonating of absence.[74]

---

[71] Among others, Ihab Hassan, "POSTmodernISM: A Paracritical Bibliography" [1971], in: Lawrence Cahoone (ed.), *From Modernism to Postmodernism: An Anthology* (Cambridge: Blackwell, 1996), p. 382-400; "The Question of Postmodernism", *Bucknell Review* 25:2, 1980, p. 117-26; "Pluralism in Postmodern Perspective", *Critical Inquiry* 12, 1985/86, p. 503-520.

[72] cf. Hassan, "Pluralism in Postmodern Perspective", p. 504.

[73] cf. ibid, p. 505.

[74] cf. ibid, p. 505.

4. *Irony*. "In absence of a cardinal principle or paradigm, we turn to play, interplay, (...), self-reflection--in short to irony. This irony assumes indeterminacy, multivalence; it aspires to clarity, the clarity of demystification, the pure light of absence. (...) Irony, perspectivism, reflexiveness: these express the ineluctable recreations of mind in search of a truth that continually eludes it, leaving it with only an ironic access or excess of self-consciousness."[75] "Irony becomes radical self-consuming play, entropy of meaning."[76]

5. *Hybridization*, or the "mutant replication of genres [such as the detective story], including parody, travesty, pastiche." Re-presentation instead of presentation and the "de-defintion" of cultural genres, hence, for instance, a blending of elements from trivial and high-brow literature.[77]

6. *Performance, Participation*. Indeterminacy elicits participation; gaps must be filled. The postmodern text, verbal or nonverbal, invites performance: it wants to be written, revised, answered, acted out.[78] Auster's postmodern detective fiction invites the reader to participate not only in finding the culprit or solving the case, but as the stories unfold and as it becomes obvious that frequentyl there is no case at all, the reader is invited to participate in filling the gaps by solving the text itself, or even more precisely, the relation between text and intertext [cf. especially ch. 7 on intertextuality].

In an essay from 1980, Hassan produced a comparative list of aspects that hint at certain characteristics of postmodernism. This paper focuses on the following: the notion of *chance, deconstruction*, the relation between *text and intertext*, the focus on the *signifier* instead of the signified, *anti-narrative*, and *absence*.[79]

In his first essay on the subject, Hassan presented a listing of elements and influences that suggest a turn from modernism to postmodernism: *Urbanism* (as a modernist rubric) is dealt with in postmodernism in terms of "the City and also the Global Village"[80]; "*dehumanization*' (...) means the end of the old Realism (...); it requires a revision of the literary and authorial Self evidenced: (...) in postmodernism

---

[75] ibid, p. 506.
[76] Hassan, "POSTmodernISM", p. 397.
[77] Hassan, "Pluralism in Postmodern Perspective ", p. 507.
[78] ibid, p. 507.
[79] cf. Hassan, "The Question of Postmodernism", p. 123
[80] Hassan, "POSTmodernISM", p. 396.

(...) by authorial self-reflexiveness, by the fusion of fact and fiction[81] (...), by things falling apart."[82]

Intertextuality is the final postmodern element that is important with regard to the discussion of Auster's NYT as postmodern detective fiction. The term 'intertextuality' has been coined by postmodern critics (among others Julia Kristeva and Roland Barthes) but is much older than postmodernism and is in fact a "phenomenon which is to be found in the literature of all ages, and most of the forms of intertextuality--which include imitation, parody, travesty, translation, adaptation, quotation, and allusion have existed ever since antiquity."[83] In his essay, Ulrich Broich refers to such 'ancient' authors as Vergil, Alexander Pope and Henry Fielding even though they employed intertextual methods for mimetic reasons by imitating the classics and thus being closer to nature.

Postmodern artists and critics, however, have used intertextuality in a radically different manner, rather like a "mosaic of quotations"[84] or a "chambre d'èchos."[85] Bloom writes that "any poem is an inter-poem and any reading of a poem is an inter-reading."[86] He further claims that "there are no texts but only relationships between texts"[87]. A distinction between intertextual and non-intertextual texts is neither relevant nor intended by postmodernism, since every text can only be an absorption and a transformation of another text and since every word refers to another word and so on.[88] Broich claims that out of this a most radical concept of 'text' could be drawn, namely that there is no 'reality' outside textuality since everything is (inter-) text, referring to Derrida's concept of "hors texte." Jorge Luis Borges' idea of the "Library of Babel,"[89] the universal library, outside which there is nothing, inside which there is everything is taken up by Paul Auster in *City of Glass* with the concept of THE TOWER OF BABEL. Above that, many of Auster's characters leave the textual and enter the 'real' world as well as the other way round.

---

[81] ibid, p. 397f.

[82] ibid, p. 400.

[83] Ulrich Broich, "Intertextuality", in: Hans Bertens and Douwe Fokkema, *International Postmodernism: Theory and Literary Practice* (Amsterdam: John Benjamins, 1997), p. 249.

[84] Julia Kristeva, *Sèmeiotikè: Récherche pour une sémanalyse* (Paris: Seuil, 1969), p. 146.

[85] Roland Barthes, *Roland Barthes par Roland Barthes* (Paris: Seuil, 1975), p. 78.

[86] Harold Bloom, *Poetry and Repression* (New Haven: Yale University Press, 1976), p. 2.

[87] Harold Bloom, *A Map of Misreading* (New York: Oxford University Press, 1975), p. 3.

[88] cf. ibid, p. 250f.

[89] Jorge Luis Borges, *Ficciones: Obras Completas 1923-1972* (Buenos Aires: Emecé, 1974), pp. 465-471.

Auster plays with intertextuality by introducing milestones of American literary history in his novels and by naming his characters after well-known fictional characters or real persons. This paper further analyzes these aspects in chapter 7.

Finally, we can summarise that the NYT can be regarded as postmodern fiction, as it fits into Linda Hutcheon's understanding of "historiographic metafiction." The trilogy is about

> issues such as those of narrative form, of intertextuality, of strategies of representation, of the role of language, of the relation between historical fact and experiental event, and, in general, of the epistemological and ontological consequences of the act of rendering problematic that which was once taken for granted by historiography--and literature.[90]

The theoretical part of this paper concludes by placing Paul Auster within the 'postmodern family'. This fact accounts for the motivations behind his work and especially behind the NYT, and strengthens the hypothesis in placing Auster and his trilogy in the genre of postmodern detective fiction. One could argue that such a brief theoretical elaboration of the rather complex question of postmodernism does not suffice. But is it not true that "to theorize postmodernism (...) is to change its character in the making no less than to acknowledge its errancies and vexations?"[91]

> Detective fiction has its norms; to 'develop' them is also to disappoint them; to 'improve' upon detective fiction is to write 'literature', not detective fiction.
> --Tzevtan Todorov--

2.2 Postmodernism and Paul Auster

If we follow Todorov's argument of the irrevocable discrepancy between detective fiction and literature, then Paul Auster seems to have contradicted himself by writing the NYT. He has written a piece of 'high' literature that is at first glance plain detective fiction, which was generally considered to be trivial literature until its

---

[90] Linda Hutcheon, *A Poetics of Postmodernism: History, Theory, Fiction* (New York: Routledge, 1988), p. xii.
[91] Hassan, "Pluralism in Postmodern Perspective", p. 504.

postmodern subversion. Auster succeeds in combining traditional elements of the Poesque story with postmodern subjectivities and a sufficient realism to lift the genre onto a higher literary plane. "At its best, detective fiction can be one of the purest and most engaging forms of storytelling. The idea that every sentence counts, that every word can make a difference--it creates a tremendous narrative propulsion. It's on that level that the form has been most interesting to me."[92] The NYT operates by creating a surface mystery in which the reader is engaged and then deviates from some of the conventions found in classical detective fiction to branch off into deeper mysteries than the ones presented on the surface. Could it not also be a "critique of the oversimplified solutions crime fiction has led us to expect, or a demonstration that the epistemological uncertainties of modern experience are best approached through formulas that do at least expect us to view life chiefly as a mystery"?[93] Auster himself comments on that aspect: "I was using those elements for many different ends (...), to get to another place, another place altogether (...), [to] the question of who is who and whether or not we are who we think we are. (...) Mystery novels always give answers; my work is about asking questions."[94]

In early postmodernism, 'realism' and 'experiment' could not have been imagined together. According to the postmodern consensus of refusing narrative, realism expressed everything postmodernism did not want to be associated with. But, as Malcolm Bradbury points out, "they ['realism' and 'experiment'] now increasingly engage in peaceful intercourse and profitable trade,"[95] of which the NYT is a good example. At the center of Auster's writing is a "preoccupation with the possibilities of telling, of making a de facto 'reality' that can meld with the reality we otherwise know."[96] It is important to mention that Paul Auster is a postmodern writer with a stronger bondage to philosophy (especially French philosophy) than to politics. He concentrates on such philosophical notions as truth, the nature of belief and knowledge, the question of meaning and identity in our society, which are often

---

[92] Paul Auster, *The Art of Hunger: Essays, Prefaces, Interviews* (Los Angeles: Sun & Moon Press, 1992), p. 257.
[93] Martin Priestman, *Crime Fiction: From Poe to the Present* (Plymouth: Northcote, 1998), p. 65.
[94] ibid, p. 261f.
[95] Malcolm Bradbury, *The Modern American Novel* (Oxford: Oxford University Press, [2]1992), p. 257.
[96] Robert Creeley, "Austerities", *Review of Contemporary Fiction* 14:1, 1994, p. 35.

triggered by his own personal experiences, may they be good or bad. In an interview, Paul Auster himself underlines that

> at bottom, I think, my work has come out of a position of intense personal despair, a very deep nihilism and hopelessness about the world, the fact of our own transcience and mortality, the inadequacy of language, the isolation of one person from another. And yet, at the same time, I've wanted to express the beauty and extraordinary happiness of feeling yourself alive, of breathing in the air, the joy of being alive in your own skin.[97]

Auster's books are postmodern in the sense that they are clearly reflexive fictions about fictions. References to other works of literature and descriptions of actual historiographic figures and events are woven into the intertextual and self-referential nature of Auster's texts. "Paul" appears in the NYT as a character, who is a writer, mistaken for a detective. So far so good. But isn't he at the same time the narrator of his own fiction? Or rather the author? Or can we still talk about any author(ity) after the "death of God" (Nietzsche) and the "death of the author" (Barthes)? This paper draws some conclusions on these questions.

Auster's fiction is one of displacement, in which chance, disappearance and a fundamental solitude of the self, which is mostly created by the indeterminacy of language as our relation to the world, play an important role. His work is strongly autobiographical and this sometimes so obvious that we sense the irony and the artful, postmodern employment in it. "It's a kind of fictitious subterranean autobiography, an attempt to imagine what my life would have been like (...). That's why I had to appear in the book as myself, but at the same time Auster is also Quinn [the detective in *City of Glass*], but in a different universe."[98] But yet, we have to be careful with such categories as autobiography and memoir, because Auster only uses personal experiences to point to certain questions, paradoxes and mysteries in our world, perhaps questions that we all wonder about. He introduces the possibility of a 'disguised' and 'alienated' autobiography and plays with it in various ways. He invites the reader to participate in the game of hide and seek, of reading and writing, of detecting who could be the author(ity) of the book. Again, Auster is willing to come up with an explanation of his own procedures.

> I wanted to implicate myself in the machinery of the book. I don't mean my autobiographical self, I mean my author self, that mysterious other who lives inside me

---

[97] Mark Irwin, "Memory's Escape: Inventing the *Music of Chance*--A Conversation with Paul Auster", *Denver Quarterly* 28:3, 1994, p. 118.
[98] Auster, *The Art of Hunger*, p. 260.

and puts my name on the covers of books. What I was hoping to do, in effect, was to take my name off the cover and put it inside the story. I wanted to open up the process, to break down walls, to expose the plumbing. There's a strange kind of trickery involved in the reading and writing of novels, after all. You see Leo Tolstoy's name on the cover of *War and Peace*, but once you open the book, Leo Tolstoy disappears. It's as though no one has really written the words you're reading. I find this 'no one' terribly fascinating --for there's finally a profound truth to it. On the one hand it's an illusion: on the other hand, it has everything to do with how stories are written. For the author of a novel can never be sure where any of it comes from. The self that exists in the world-- the self whose name appears on the covers of books--is finally not the same who writes the book.[99]

Auster's fiction is a unique and important synthesis of postmodern concerns, 'experimental realism' (Jerome Klinkowitz)[100], as well as social and philosophical questions. In the light of everything that has been mentioned above, we can now turn to the text itself, the trilogy, written by the 'postmodern realist' Paul Auster.

---

[99] ibid, p. 293.
[100] quoted in: Bradbury, p. 257.

Chance is part of reality.
--Paul Auster--

3 Chance, Truth, and Meaning: The World(s) of the Detective- The Detective in the World(s), or Will he solve the case?

The real mysteries in the NYT are the protagonists themselves, and the novels become inquiries into the human subject. I will introduce and characterise the true protagonists of every detective story, namely the detectives Quinn, Blue and the nameless narrator and their place in the world(s). Auster's stories differ from the classical and the hard-boiled detective story in their character development and character motivation. We learn a great deal more about the principal characters in Auster's postmodern novels than we do about Chandler's romantic-at-heart and heroic knight Marlowe, a man who has to go "down these mean streets," or about Poe's superintellectual Dupin, since in these stories, action is privileged over characterisation. Quinn in the *City of Glass* and Blue in *Ghosts* are also motivated by justice and self-sacrifice, but they push it to a ridiculous level. The reason they do so is, however, ultimately not out of concern for others or some innate sense of duty, rather Quinn and Blue regard their jobs as escape mechanisms. Quinn avoids thinking about his own existence by dedicating himself to the Stillman case. Similarly, Blue is very diligent regarding his work, but he too seeks to escape the responsibilities of his own life. The nameless narrator is out to solve the case of finding his suddenly disappeared friend Fanshawe, in order to find himself, in order to find truth and meaning in *his* world(s).

As a postmodern writer, Auster is not willing to offer us one coherent world, but rather 'layers' of overlapping worlds, in which the characters and hence the readers have to find their way. The book turns both outward towards the world and inward towards the self. The detective himself is yet more unconventional. Possessing all of the marginality, but none of the self-confidence of the classic detective, he spends much of his time walking in circles through the streets of New York, adopting roles for himself to boost his confidence, or stepping into roles suggested for him by others, gladly taking on new identities. In a 'city of glass', his 'world(s)' seem to become transparent; yet, what is revealed is not some hidden truth, or the answer to his epistemological questions, but rather the fragility of his world(s), the fragility of meaning, the epistemological fallibility of our postmodern times. The plurality of worlds, of identities in different worlds--fictional or 'real'--and of "things and events that have their place in two or more overlapping worlds can simultaneously be true and untrue, depending on the world within which such statements are made."[101]

We find the following confrontations among the different worlds of the NYT: There is a clear confrontation between the novel's fictional world and 'real'-world historical facts, persons and events. A few examples will clarify that point. In CoG, the best example is Paul Auster himself. Not only does he appear as a character in the novel, Quinn's life in many ways also resembles Auster's real life. Quinn is the same age as Auster when he wrote *City of Glass*, and he also lost his wife and son. At that time, Auster had been divorced from his first wife. Their mutual son bears the same name as Quinn: Daniel. Auster's second wife is called Siri, and so is the wife of the character Auster in the novel. Through the parallels with which Quinn and Auster are connected, Auster partly fictionalises himself. Hence, we have three Austers: author, narrator, and character, each ontologically different. But is Auster the author(ity) of the text? From the links between Quinn and the fictitious Auster, and the real author Auster, Martin Klepper comes to the following result.

> Im fiktionalen Auster und in Quinn hat sich der Autor durch eine Art ontologische Zellteilung gedoppelt: einmal als 'ganzer' Charakter, der ein erfülltes Familienleben führt und keinen Verlust kennt, und einmal als gebrochener Charakter, der nach dem Verlust von Frau und Sohn durch seine Versprachlichungen seine Einheit wiederherstellen will. Durch die metafiktionale Doppelung fließt der 'Text' von Anbeginn über den Rand des Romans hinaus, saugt die Wirklichkeit in seine Textualität hinein. [102]

---

[101] Hans Bertens, "The Detective", in: Hans Bertens and Douwe Fokkema, *International Postmodernism: Theory and Literary Practice* (Amsterdam: John Benjamins, 1997), pp. 195ff .

[102] Martin Klepper, *Pynchon, Auster, DeLillo: Die amerikanische Postmoderne zwischen Spiel und Rekonstruktion* (Frankfurt: Campus, 1996), p. 255.
(By means of an ontological cell division, the author has 'doubled' himself in the fictional Auster and in Quinn: first, as a 'whole' character, leading a harmonious and fulfilling family life and not knowing any loss, and secondly, as a 'broken' character, striving to reestablish his identity through his *Versprachlichungen* after the experience of having lost his wife and son. Due to metafictional doubling, the 'text' is flowing beyond the boundaries of the novel from its very beginning, thus absorbing reality in its own textuality). [My translation]

Auster also introduces Cervantes into the novel. At the beginning, an allusion to Cervantes is found in the character of Michael Saavedra, the person who recommended the detective Paul Auster to Peter and Virginia Stillman. Mrs. Saavedra, his wife, is the nurse of Peter Stillman Jr. Of course, Cervantes, the author of *Don Quixote* bears the full name of Miguel de Cervantes Saavedra. Cervantes and his book are mentioned again in the meeting between Quinn and Auster. A variety of other real persons and events (Poe, Hawthorne, Whitman, Kaspar Hauser, Thoreau, Melville, as well as childhood events of Auster and other metafictional devices) are visible throughout the trilogy and will be dealt with in detail in the chapters on author(ity) and intertextuality. Brian McHale's words about Umberto Eco's *The Name of the Rose*, resemble in many ways Auster's orientation and the results for the reader. "This queasiness of ours is precisely an ontological queasiness, a symptom of our uncertainty about the exact boundaries between historical fact and fiction in the text."[103]

The 'world' in postmodern detective fiction lacks order, stability, continuity, necessity, and coherence. The settings are fluid, and the chain of events is the product of hazard and circumstance. It is not a world that lends itself to rational inquiry. Even if the decentered world of detective fiction may finally hang together or cohere, it does not, however, really make sense. Auster writes in *The Invention of Solitude*: "As in the meanings of words, things take on meaning only in relationship to each other."[104] However, if one may now draw the conclusion that in a postmodern detective story there is almost *no* relationship between things (or clues), there will consequently be no relationship between the different 'worlds', in which Auster's writer-detectives blindly move along. Such a destabilisation of the projected world(s), the fictional and the 'real', in which the detectives have to execute their quest for meaning and truth, is caused by Auster's strategy of *mise-en-abyme*, or the "paradoxical reproduction *within* the fictional world *of* the fictional world itself."[105] In CoG, Auster's examination of *Don Quixote* by the fictional Auster in the novel stands for the novel as a whole, and thus self-reflexively repeats itself in the novel.

---

[103] Brian McHale, *Constructing Postmodernism* (London: Routledge, 1992), p. 150.
[104] Paul Auster, *The Invention of Solitude* (London: Faber and Faber, 1988), p. 161.
[105] McHale, p. 153.

The same holds true for Thoreau's *Walden* in *Ghosts*, or the film *Out of the Past*, and the semi-fictional biography of Fanshawe in *The Locked Room*.

Finally, there is the issue of closure to consider, or rather the lack of it in the postmodern detective story. The collage of images, mediums, and genres inherent in postmodernism together with the ambiguity and uncertainty in the postmodern world combine to create a multiplicity of possibilities and outcomes for the self. Following this ambiguity, there are texts which are left open-ended and subject to interpretation. Resolution is not clear-cut because postmodern writers are attempting to accurately reflect the indeterminacy, uncertainty--the continous change of possibilities--prevalent in these postmodern times. Auster is one of those artists who seems reluctant to bring a full and tidy resolution to his narratives. Instead he gives us "open-ended endings". The mysteries, on the surface and the underlying deeper ones, are left unresolved or full of holes. By leaving Quinn in a traumatised uncertain state when we last see him, by leaving Blue's fate uncertain, and by leaving the nameless narrator in turmoil, Auster moves away from the satisfying closure of the classical and hard-boiled school towards a more problematic, yet also more realistic ending of our postmodern times. Let us have a look in detail.

3.1 Quinn

In *City of Glass*, Daniel Quinn (he shares his initials with Don Quixote, a fact that will be of more importance later), a writer of detective novels under the Poesque pseudonym William Wilson, is called by a man who mistakes him for Paul Auster, a detective. After a second and a third call, Quinn assumes Auster's identity and accepts the case, which involves him in keeping an eye on Peter Stillman Sr, who has just been released from prison after serving a long sentence, and in protecting Stillman's son Peter Stillman Jr. against any evil intentions his father may have in mind. As it turns out, the case comes to nothing. Peter Stillman Sr. is rather harmless, suddenly disappears and Quinn slowly loses the grip over his life and his existence. The Paul Auster in the novel turns out to be a writer rather than a detective. Quinn desperately tries to make sense out of a senseless case, spends his days watching the apartment of Stillman Jr and his wife, who seem to have vanished as well, and, in the course of his long observation, loses his own apartment and decides to stay in the Stillman's house. He spends his days naked in an empty room (copying Peter Stillman Jr.'s horrible experience as a child of being held in a dark room for nine years without being able to talk to anybody, so that his father may thus discover God's language) filling the red notebook he had bought earlier to record his observations with an ever widening range of material. Inexplicably, the days shorten rapidly, and he can complete no more than a couple of sentences before it gets dark again. When there are no more pages of the red notebook to be filled, Quinn completely disappears. Paul Auster and a friend, who later claims to have narrated the story, only find the red notebook with which the story of Quinn is then reconstructed.

The narrator of *City of Glass* tells the reader that "it was a wrong number that started it", then proceeds to explain that "as for Quinn, (...) who he was, where he came from, and what he did are of no great importance" (3), implying that, as in the classical detective story, our investigator's past and present life are not as important as the mystery that will soon unfold. However, this is deceptive, because very soon we learn a great deal more about him and the world he exists in: how he was once a more ambitious and prolific writer who produced more than the single detective novel he now publishes once a year; how since the death of his wife and son, Quinn has retreated into an anonymous life, having lost all his friends; how "more than anything else (...) what he liked to do was walk" (4) in New York, "an inexhaustible space, a labyrinth of endless steps" because "no matter how far he walked, no matter how well he came to know its neighborhoods and streets, it always left him with the feeling of being lost. Lost not only in the city, but within himself as well" (4). Through his endless walks, he is able to obliterate memory and thinking, he is "giving himself up to the movements of the streets, (...) reducing himself to a seeing eye" and this, "more than anything else, brought him a measure of peace, a salutary emptiness within. The world was outside of him, around him, before him" (4), but it did not reach him inside, thus making it impossible for him "to dwell on any thing for very long" (4). Watching his idol William "Mookie" Wilson (yes, another one of those Wilsons) in endless baseball games on TV, going to the opera and walking, help him to shut off his thinking, to forget who he was, or maybe who he was not.

All he ever asked for was "to be nowhere" (4). Before a "part of him had died" (4), Quinn used to write "several books of poetry, (...) plays, critical essays, and had worked on a long number of translations" (5), forms of writing which forced him to be critical about the world, about the people he was surrounded by and which he had published under his own name and identity, Daniel Quinn. Writing detective novels allows Quinn to check out of his subjectivity, be his fictional private eye Max Work, and live in the world of the detective. The involvement in the Stillmann case provides him with yet another form of escape, he 'becomes' Paul Auster, the detective, the only difference being that he is now out in the 'real' world and not in the fictional world of detective novels. He believes that the impersonation enables him to enter the world of his favorite fictional form--mystery fiction. He likes mystery novels because their worlds are characterised by 'plenitude and economy'.

> In the good mystery there is nothing wasted, no sentence, no word that is not significant. And even if it is not siginificant, it has the potential to be so--which amounts to the same thing. The world of the book comes to life, seething with possibilities, with secrets and contradictions. Since everything seen or said, even the slightest most trivial thing, can bear a connection to the outcome of the story, nothing must be overlooked. Everything becomes essence; the center of the book shifts with each event that propels it forward (15).

Quinn here singles out the essential features of the world in mystery and detective fiction. It is a centered world, full of significance and coherence. This is the kind of world Quinn longs to occupy, if only because his personal life is so painful. One critic observes that "for him, the detective story is a refuge from the metaphysical chaos he finds around him."[106] He slowly seems to learn how to play detective. In a very 'Chandler-like' scene in the Stillman's apartment Quinn feels like Marlowe, "He was warming up now. Something had told him that he had captured the right tone, and a sudden sense of pleasure surged trough him, as though he had just managed to cross some internal border within himself" (41). But "crossing the border" turns out to become his major problem. The longer the case goes on, the less Quinn is able to distinguish between the fictional and the 'real' world. Usually, the "detective is one who looks, listens, who moves through this morass of objects and events in search of the thought, the idea that will pull all these things together and make sense of them" (9), and Quinn is fascinated by such skill. Yet, his own lack of detective skills and

---

[106] Norma Rowen, "The Detective in Search of the Lost Tongue of Adam", p. 226.

his inexperience in criminal issues lead him into a state of continuing frustration since "like most people, Quinn knew almost nothing about crime. He had never murdered anyone, had never stolen anything, and he did not know anyone who had. (...) Whatever he knew about these things, he had learned from books, films and newspapers" (8). Quinn plays Auster so well, that he feels reluctant to abandon the character as the case progresses, but he soon finds himself unable to read Stillman as easily as his own Max Work:

> Quinn was deeply disillusioned. He had always imagined that the key to good detective work was a close observation of details. The more accurate the scrutiny, the more successful the results. The implication was that human behavior could be understood, that beneath the infinite facade of gestures, tics and silences, there was finally a coherence, an order, a source of motivation (80).

Quinn is searching for a city of glass, a world of transparency, in which there is a "correspondence between signifiers and signifieds."[107] He does, however, only find himself in a world of mirrors and multiplicity, in which signs are purely arbitrary. Earlier in the novel, when Quinn is looking for Stillman who arrives at the train station in New York, he first seems to have found the right man, when suddenly another man stopped "directly behind Stillman" (67), whose "face was the exact twin of Stillman's" (68). Quinn doesn't know which one to follow. "Whatever choice he made (...) would be arbitrary, a submission to chance. Uncertainty would haunt him to the end" (68). The possibility of total knowledge and coherence is thus obliterated. "There was no way to know: not this, not anything" (68). From the very beginning of the case, Quinn finds himself in a world of chance. How would the story proceed if Quinn had followed the other 'Stillman'? How can he be certain that his Stillman is the right one? Of course, the answer is, that he will never know. Another example of Quinn's dilemma is Stillman's behavior of wandering through New York and collecting debris which he then dutifully records in a red notebook (one of several red notebooks that appear in the NYT) and puts in an old-fashioned carpet bag; a behavior that seems entirely arbitrary. In this world actions can no longer be 'read', activity can no longer be plotted, because signifiers have become detached from signifieds; the whole idea of motivation has been undermined. But Quinn refuses to relinquish the idea of motivation. Consulting his own notes, he draws maps detailing

---

[107] Alison Russel, "Deconstructing the *New York Trilogy*", p. 72.

the course of each of Stillman's daily walks and discovers that each daily ramble spells a letter when drawn out on a piece of paper. When he arranges the letters in their daily chronological order they spell out OWER OF BAB, which, if "making all due allowances for the fact that he had missed the first four days and that Stillman had not yet finished" (85), then results in THE TOWER OF BABEL, seemingly connecting Stillman's activities with his dissertation on the prelapsarian language of God spoken in paradise. "It seemed to him that he was looking for a sign. He was ransacking the chaos of Stillman's movements for some glimmer of cogency. This implied only one thing: that he continued to disbelieve the arbitrariness of Stillman's actions. He wanted there to be a sense to them, no matter how obscure" (109). He tries to rely on his own creation Max Work, a detective who reasons, who fulfills Poe's characteristics of the good detective in being succesful in the "identification of the reasoner's intellect with that of his opponent" (48), the cool hard-boiled warrior, of which Quinn thinks when he is in the Stillman apartment for the first time. "[Quinn] thought about what Max Work might have been thinking, had he been there. He decided to light a cigarette. He blew the smoke into the room" (17). But Quinn is simply not able to properly do his detective work. He refuses to believe that Stillman Sr. has abandoned his crazy scheme, that he will not try to kill his son, and that he is, after all, just a very disturbed old man. However, if Quinn accepted this fact, it would mean giving up the guise of Paul Auster and returning to being himself. So he elects to ignore it.

Quinn's "mystery" world totally unravels when Stillman Sr. disappears, at the end of the day on which he presumably finishes spelling out his secret message. (Auster tells Quinn several months later that Stillman killed himself that evening by jumping from the Brooklyn Bridge.) With Stillman out of the picture, Quinn no longer has a suspect, a plot, or an assignment. He has reached ground zero: "Quinn was nowhere now. He had nothing, he knew nothing, he knew that he knew nothing" (159). Quinn cannot reach Virginia Stillman to tell her that he has lost the trail of her husband's father and, despite the fact that the Stillman's telephone line is busy for over a day, he never makes an attempt to go to their apartment to see if they are alright. He clings to the idea of motivation: "The busy signal had not been arbitrary. It had been a sign, and it was telling him that he could not yet break his connection with the case" (169). He thus converts contingency into fate, chance into destiny. Instead he reasons:

> Ideally, an operative should maintain close contact with his clients. That had always been one of Max Work's principles. But was it really neccessary? As long as Quinn did his job, how could it matter? If there were any misunderstandings, surely they could be cleared up, once the case was settled. He could proceed, then, as he wished. (...) From now on there would be no stopping him. (...) Quinn stepped across to the other side [of the Stillman's street], found a spot for himself in a narrow alleyway, and settled in for the night (134).

Quinn has grown so enamored of the case and the false identity that came with it that he is reluctant to see it end. He projects himself in yet another world, the world of the constant vigilant who slowly transforms himself into a bum who lives in a garbage box. However, this is again only the surface, the 'outer' world. Quinn still seems to cling to the pretense that he is doing a job for the Stillmans, but his intended motives stray away from the real condition, in which Quinn finds himself: "He spent many hours looking up at the sky" (140), instead of intensely watching the apartment; and what he really strives for is best expressed earlier in the novel, when Quinn listens to a street clarinetist whose music "went on and on, always finally the same, and yet the longer I listened the harder I found it to leave. To be inside that music, to be drawn into the circle of its repetitions: perhaps that is a place where one could finally disappear" (130). Or maybe put in a different way by quoting Baudelaire: "Wherever I am not is the place where I am myself (...), or else, (...) anywhere out of the world" (132).

Quinn's wish is granted at the end of the book, as he begins to dissipate, but there he realises (for the first time, it seems) that writing could have functioned as well as the clarinet music: that writing could have given him the power to dissipateand thus to disappear if he had done more of it. Quinn 'used' his writing only as a way to bring in money, instead of comprehending that writing can function both as an outlet for self-discovery and as an escape mechanism. Quinn could only exist within a textual world, which would enable him to make sense of the 'real' world (or the case, whichever we may prefer) by projecting it and himself into the process of writing and text. Quinn, however, sees the boundaries between these two worlds violated and can no longer distinguish between them. At the end, it is too late. When he finishes writing in the red notebook, he will cease to be. He has finally stepped into the state of non-being that he always sought and he

> regretted having wasted so many pages at the beginning of the red notebook, and in fact felt sorry that he had bothered to write about the Stillman case at all. For the case was far behind him now, and he no longer bothered to think about it. It had been a bridge to another place in his life, and now that he had crossed it, its meaning had been lost (156).

The meaning, which temporarily seems to have been determined by the Stillman case, has been lost again. He now seeks meaning in "another place", in writing. Yet, the problem for Quinn is now that he is running out of pages in the notebook. If writing is what is sustaining his existence in the place "where one could finally disappear", he worries about what will happen when he runs out of ink and paper.

> He wondered if he had it in him to write without a pen, if he could learn to speak instead, filling the darkness with his voice, speaking the words into thin air, into the walls, into the city, even if the light never came back again. The last sentence of the red notebook reads: 'What will happen when there are no more pages in the red notebook?' (156f).

What happens is not exactly clear, but Quinn has been "disconnected" (146) from the narrative just like the Stillman's telephone. One question, however, remains. What are we to make of all that? The case has not been solved, all the main characters, including the protagonist, the writer-turned-detective Quinn, have disappeared from the scenery. Stillman Sr. has committed suicide and the young Stillman together with his wife last appear on page 79, only halfway through the novel. Was it all a big conspiracy, in which Quinn had to play a certain role (Oedipa Maas says hello)? Has Stillman succeeded in killing the couple before he said good-bye to this world without Quinn having noticed it? Has there really ever been a crime? Auster confronts us, in true postmodern fashion, with an open-ended ending that leaves us in the 'heart of darkness', in which we have followed Quinn during his quest for knowledge and meaning in the world. By the way, a detective named Daniel Quinn appears in the third novel of the trilogy, *The Locked Room*, in which he is hired by Fanshawe's wife to track down her missing husband. However again--if this is actually the same Quinn, something Auster does not make clear, creating more and more 'postmodern' disorder and indeterminacy--he does not even come close to any satisfying solution. In *City of Glass*, the mystery he investigates he creates rather than solves. The real mystery is one of a confused writer-detective, who descends into a labyrinth in which fact and fiction become increasingly difficult to separate and in which at the end his existence is reduced to nothingness. Quinn is no more than a white spot in the universe, no longer distinguishable from any other spot. When he goes back, after his failure to wrap up the case, to the scene where his assignment began, he finds it "stripped bare, and the rooms now held nothing. Each one was identical to every other: a wooden floor and four white walls" (151). Likewise, the final image of the city is one in which the landscape threatens to white out, to be reduced to a blank: "The city was entirely white now, and the snow kept falling, as though it would never end" (158).

3.2 Blue

Ghosts, the second novel of the trilogy, also depicts one man hiring another to follow a third; the story's aggressively abstract nature is reflected in the fact that all its characters are named for colors: "First of all there is Blue. Later there is White, and then there is Black, and before the beginning there is Brown" (162). The connection between them is something like that: Blue, a student of Brown, has been hired by White to spy on Black. Later we meet Green, Grey, Gold, Red (a bartender) and Violet (a blowsy tart). The mystery does not take place so much within the story as on some higher level. How much higher the level is, is, in fact, very much part of the mystery. Again, we leave the stronghold of realistic perception that there is one world, which we can rely on. Right at the beginning, the narrator adresses the reader, informing us how the story will proceed before we have any clue what is going to happen.

> Little does Blue know, of course, that the case will go on for years. But the present is no less dark than the past, and its mystery is equal to anything the future might hold. Such is the way of the world: one step at a time, one wor[l]d and then the next. There are certain things that Blue cannot possibly know at this point. For knowledge comes slowly, and when it comes, it is often at great personal expense (162f).

Should we avoid the conclusion that all this stands for something? Or nothing? Are we to read the story as a quest for knowledge, for meaning? Or are we being asked to read the story as a fable, a metaphor and not to submerge ourselves in this story, to believe in its reality? Are we not, in fact, being asked to stay above it, to approach the story with the question 'what does it all mean'? The story seems to be a mere construct of a story: the characters speak without quotation marks; we encounter a deliberate minimalism at work, everything is stripped down to its bare facts, almost in the same way as a classical detective story, in which only the case, the process of detection and the solution are of any importance. But who is Blue? In what world(s) does he live? Does the outside world make sense? Or do we have to choose either between an outer and an inner world to be able to know what it all means? What is the story? And will we get the answer of what it is supposed to mean?

As mentioned above, a certain detective Blue is hired by White to shadow Black. The narrator says the location is unimportant, "let's say Brooklyn Heights, for the sake of argument. Some quiet, rarely traveled street not far from the bridge-- Orange Street perhaps" (163). Blue moves into the third-floor of a four-story brownstone to shadow Black, who lives in a third-floor apartment opposite (William Wilson, Quinn's pseudonym in *City of Glass* and the original character created by Poe could not have mirrored himself better than Blue and Black). Like the hard-boiled detective, Blue is visited by his client in his office, then going undercover, he says goodbye to the future Mrs. Blue and out he is to do his job. Although he misses her right from the beginning he hesitates to call her, since "the man must always be the stronger one" (165). Blue is a detective self-conscious about his social role. He reads *True Detective* and *Stranger than Fiction* with devotion. Owing to a peculiarity of his client, Blue is consigned to remain in his room and write weekly reports, which he mails to White. Instead of a writer, who turns into a detective like Quinn, we meet a detective, who turns into a writer. Observing Black, Blue notes that Black is composing a manuscript. Hence, Blue spends his days writing a report about someone who spends his days writing. It is a job that Blue, who "likes to be up and about, moving from one place to another, doing things" (166), comes to loathe because it allows him far too much time to think. "I'm not the Sherlock Holmes type, he would say to Brown, whenever the boss gave him a particular sedentary task. Give me something I can sink my teeth into" (166). The case demands that Blue do something he has never done before: attempt to think and reason exactly like his 'enemy' in order to come to a close approximation of his thoughts; a Dupin-like skill.

These mental exercises eventually begin to cause a change within Blue and make him invest more time thinking than he ever has before.

> For the first time in his life, he finds that he has been thrown back on himself, with nothing to grab hold of, nothing to distinguish one moment from the next. He has never given much thought to the world inside him, and though he always knew it was there, it has remained an unknown quantity, unexplored and therefore dark, even to himself. (...) He has always taken pleasure in the world as such, asking no more of things than that they be there. And until now they have been, etched vividly against the daylight, distinctly telling him what they are, so perfectly themselves and nothing else that he has never had to pause before them or look twice. Now, suddenly, with the world as it were removed from him (...) he finds himself thinking about things that have never ocurred to him before (171).

Blue begins a slow and painful existential investigation as he scrutinises his own world. Again, we are far away from normal detective work, no crime seems to be at hand, the case seems to go on and on. The world around him, which he used to know so well, becomes more and more frightening, dark, uncertain and plural; it seems to lose its sense, on which he so strongly had relied on before the case started. He realises that Black is not only writing, but also reading a book, "Walden by Henry David Thoreau [published by Walter J. Black, Inc.!). Blue has never heard of it before and writes it down carefully into his notebook" (166). He starts reading the book as well but does not know what to make out of it. "As Blue begins to read, he feels as though he is entering an alien world. Trudging through swamps and brambles, hoisting himself up gloomy screes and treacherous cliffs, he feels like a prisoner on a forced march, and his only thought is to escape" (193). Blue stumbles through the geography and geology of the book without being able to understand its meaning. "What's all this about planting beans and not drinking coffee or eating meat? Why all these interminable descriptions of birds? Blue thought that he was going to get a story, or at least something like a story (...)" (194). Again, Auster confronts us with a story-within-a-story reducing Blue's existence to an ascetic condition, in which waiting, reading, writing, and most importantly thinking are the only activities Blue is able to participate in. Blue's description of Walden is self-reflexive: "There is no story, no plot, no action--nothing but a man sitting alone in a room and writing a book" (202). Blue becomes trapped in the world of the text: "How to get out of the room that is the book that will go on being written for as long as he stays in the room?" (202). He does not yet understand that he sort of relives the experiences narrated to us in *Walden*, for "knowledge comes slowly" (163).

A series of events further complicate Blue's life. He discovers that his fiancee is seeing another man. He tries to meet White in the post office, suspecting that White and Black are actually the same persons, but White eludes him. Black continues to scribble and Blue's anxiety mounts. "He has learned a thousand facts [about Black], but the only thing they have taught him is that he knows nothing. For the fact remains that none of this is possible. It is not possible for such a man as Black to exist" (203). We learn about knowledge that too much is just as dangerous as not enough. Hence, Blue knows everything about Black: when he will eat; when he will sleep; when he will go out; and when he will stay at home. Yet precisely because he knows everything, he knows nothing. Through this self-confession he denies his own knowledge and at the same time Black's existence in the world. He seems to have come to an end, "months go by, and at last he says to himself out loud: I can't breathe anymore. This is the end. I'm dying" (203). Then, Blue, who always felt more comfortable with physical activity rather than mental activity, finally decides that "the key to the case is action" (199) and proceeds to disguise himself and instigate a series of encounters with Black. These brief discussions, however, do no more than further trouble Blue, "for with each word Black speaks, he finds himself understanding less and less" (208). In one particular scene, Black even introduces himself as a private detective, whose job is to watch someone and send in a report about him every week. Nothing ever seems to happen. Hence, Paul Auster is writing about a detective turned writer who has to watch somebody who is a writer turned detective who has to hand in a weekly report about the one he is supposed to watch. Of course, the irony is self-reflexively deviated since both Blue and Black know that it is all a game. Talk about postmodern 'meta-irony'. In another scene, Blue, disguised as a brush salesman, visits Black in his apartment, describing it as a "no man's land, the place you come to at the end of the world" (220). This is the place and time, where the story comes to an end, and so does Blue's detective job, which has taken him into so many different worlds. The world of the self and the other, the world of fact and fiction, the world of the fictional ghosts Melville, Thoreau and Whitman, and the world of Black's memoirs.

"Only because he already knows" (222) now that Black has used him as a year-long witness to the writing of his memoirs (which are actually one long suicide note), does he go and break into Black's apartment where he finds the weekly reports he had been sending to White. Blue then decides to confront Black directly, knowing that he will never be able to "erase the whole story" (227) without having cleared things up between the two. As Blue enters Black's apartment, it turns out that Black has been waiting for him and threatens to kill him along with himself. Blue disarms Black and attacks him, rendering him unconscious, possibly dead. "There seems to be something [breathing], but he can't tell if it's coming from Black or himself [they have come to be so close to each other that it is almost impossible for Blue to tell the difference]. If he is alive now, Blue thinks, it won't be for long. And if he's dead, then so be it" (231). Afterward, Blue takes Black's manuscript with him, reads it, finds out that he "knew it all by heart" (232) and leaves. Black's wasted life mirrors Blue's.

This time, we seem to be rewarded for our efforts with a solution, something Blue expects from Black as well. "You're supposed to tell me the story. Isn't that how it's supposed to end? You tell me the story, and then we say good-bye" (230). Black is actually willing to explain why he needed Blue so much:

> [You] remind[ed] me of what I was supposed to be doing. Every time I looked up, you were there, watching me, following me, always in sight, boring into me with your eyes. You were the whole world to me, Blue, and I turned you into my death. You're the one thing that doesn't change, the one thing that turns everything inside out (230).

We get the answer to the questions within the story; we find out who White and Black are and what they have been up to. However, we don't get the answer to the meta-mystery. What, in fact, did it all mean? Perhaps nothing at all? If the meaning is that there is no meaning, then there is a meaning. The narrator reminds us that "the story is not yet over. There is still the final moment, and that will not come until Blue leaves the room. Such is the way of the world: Not one moment more, not one moment less. When Blue stands up from his chair, puts on his hat, and walks through the door, that will be the end of it" (232). But where exactly is he going? Is Black really dead, and has Blue's killing of Black then been the crime of the story? The ending of the story is again left open, and although the narrator tells us that "where he [Blue] goes after that is not important" (232), he even seems to struggle with the impulse to throw in a romanticised cliched ending to cap off his story:

> Anything is possible, therefore. I myself prefer to think that he went far away, boarding a train that morning and going out West to start a new life. It is even possible that America was not the end of it. In my secret dreams, I like to think of Blue booking passage on some ship and sailing to China. Let it be China, then, and we'll leave it at

that. For now is the moment that Blue stands up from his chair, puts on his hat, and walks through the door. And from this moment on, we know nothing (232).

So again, "we know nothing" and the reader's quest for knowledge has been disappointed. We leave behind a fragmented world, in which Blue has had the role of a detective that comes to understand that past actions and events are an indelible part of existence and that the postmodern self has to come to terms with a plurality of worlds. "Something happens, Blue thinks, and then it goes on happening forever. It can never be changed, can never be otherwise" (193). It is all a question of chance, and that is part of reality, part of Auster's fiction. Let the truth be chance then, and we'll leave it at that. "Whether or not it means something is not for the story to tell" (3).

3.3 The Nameless Narrator

The Locked Room, the final volume of the NYT, takes its title from a popular conventional motif of detective fiction. A dead body is discovered in a sealed room, the exits having been locked from the inside (this goes as far back as Poe's "The Muders in the Rue Morgue"). In this novel we do not have a corpse, and a locked room only appears in the final stage of the novel and inside the "skull" (345) of the narrator. Instead, we meet another writer turned detective on a quest for truth and meaning in the world; this time he does not even have a name. A transition from Quinn to Blue to the 'nameless narrator'. On the surface, the narrator seems to correspond with the image of the hard-boiled detective who shows personal interest in the case. The story is told by a first-person narrator through which the reader follows the 'case'. But again, we are not confronted with an ordinary crime or familiar detective work, but rather with the more rarified search for self. The nameless narrator, whom we are meant to identify with Mr. Auster himself (as we will see later), is not a real detective but a biographer; which is actually much the same thing: a chaser of facts, details and clues. "I was a detective, after all, and my job was to hunt for clues. Faced with a million bits of information, led down a million paths of false inquiry, I had to find the one path that would take me where I wanted to go" (332). Fanshawe, a writer, has mysteriously disappeared (Fanshawe is a direct reference to Hawthorne, as it is the title of his first novel). The narrator is contacted by Fanshawe's wife Sophie (Hawthorne's wife was called Sophia) to examine the literary work of Fanshawe, which he was never willing to publish. A friend of the narrator's in youth, Fanshawe has long been out of touch with him. On the assumption that Fanshawe is dead, the narrator agrees to become his literary executer, getting novels, plays, and poetry into print and creating Fanshawe's posthumous reputation as an important, serious writer. During the whole process of the 'Fanshawe business', the narrator and Sophie get closer to each other, and finally fall in love.

> In some sense, this is were it should end. The young genius is dead, but his work will live on, his name will be remembered for years to come. His childhood friend has rescued the beautiful young widow, and the two of them will live happily ever after. That would seem to wrap it up, with nothing left but a final curtain call. But it turns out that this is only the beginning. What I have written so far is no more than a prelude, a quick synopsis of everything that comes before the story I have to tell (278).

As we learn from the narrator, this is only the start of the story and thus of the case. It is at this point that the narrator is notified by letter that Fanshawe is still alive but wishes to remain missing. He then agrees to write Fanshawe's biography, marries Sophie, and adopts Fanshawe's son Ben, always having in mind that Fanshawe is alive. That knowledge proves dangerous. As a result he begins to lose his grip on reality. "Something monstrous was happening, and I had no control over it anymore. Thoughts stop where the world begins (...). I could no longer make the right distinctions. Apples are not oranges, peaches are not plums (...). But everything was beginning to have the same taste to me" (341/42). He gives up the study, and is subsequently summoned to the threshold of the room in which, it turns out, Fanshawe, still alive, is hiding. The doors are never opened and the two men never see one another. On his way home, the narrator reads a notebook (the third notebook in the third novel) Fanshawe has left for him that, not surprisingly, fails to clear up the fundamental mysteries of Fanshawe's existence.

The narrator faces another plurality of worlds which clearly have to do with Fanshawe's influence on him. In their early childhood, Fanshawe is a constant shadow, "he is the place where everything begins for me, and without him I would hardly know who I am" (236). Whereas the narrator was "an adolescent Sancho astride [his] donkey, watching [his] friend do battle with himself" (254) (of course, another allusion to Quixote), Fanshawe was "always standing at the exact center of things" (255). Later, their lives take different directions, "they went off to different places, drifted apart" (235) and the narrator was forced to work on his own existence and to live in his own world. And then, "out of nowhere, Fanshawe had suddenly reappeared in [his] life" (236). He is drawn into Fanshawe's past, his family, his literary work and again struggles to find his place in the world, which he often considers to be meaningless. He goes out of his way to convince himself--and the reader--that we all are subject to the whims of chance. He dredges up stories of such historical figures as La Chère, Lorenzo Da Ponte, Bakhtin or Mrs. Winchester, and his own boyhood friend Fanshawe to prove that it is fruitless to find logical patterns in our lives, and hence in our world, because "in the end, each life is no more than the sum of contingent facts, a chronicle of chance intersections, of flukes, of random events that divulge nothing but their own lack of purpose" (256). Throughout the novel he stresses that "lives make no sense (...). Every life is inexplicable. (...) A man lives and then he dies, and what happens in between makes no sense. (...) Each life is irreducible to anything other than itself. Which is as much as to say: lives make no sense" (291, 295, 298). The narrator tells himself that "lives make no sense" because to do otherwise would imply a number of painful self-admissions: that his life has come to be largely influenced and orchestrated by Fanshawe, who has the same occupation--writing.

As Fanshawe's literary executor, he takes a certain amount of credit for Fanshawe's success. "It was probably necessary for me to equate Fanshawe's success with my own" although he then realises the horrifying pun behind this appointment, namely that Fanshawe had "chosen [him] as his executioner" (317). Stephen Bernstein notes that "this discrepancy between the two tasks thrusts the narrator into his detective project, the writing of Fanshawe's biography, which is only a cover story for his own investigation into the meaning of Fanshawe's disappearance."[108] Under the pretext that he wishes to spare his wife the grief of learning that Fanshawe is alive, the narrator decides to kill Fanshawe off by writing a semi-fictional biography of his former friend, which is the text this character supposedly writes and which we read--the manuscript of TLR.

---

[108] Stephen Bernstein, "Auster's Sublime Closure: *The Locked Room*", in: Dennis Barone, *Beyond the Red Notebook*, p.90.

There was never any question of telling the truth. Fanshawe had to be dead, or else the book would make no sense. Not only would I have to leave the letter out, but I would have to pretend that it had never been written. I make no bones about what I was planning to do. It was clear to me from the beginning, and I plunged into it with deceit in my heart (291).

As the story proceeds, the writing of the biography takes complete possession of the narrator's life. He pretends to be looking for clues and connections to write about Fanshawe's life, but he is really out to track him down, to question him face to face why he had left his wife and unborn child, why he let him know that he is still alive, and to rid himself of Fanshawe's shadow, which would secure his new-found happiness with Sophie and Ben.

I no longer had any intention of writing it [the biography]. The book existed for me now only in so far as it could lead me to Fanshawe, and beyond there was no book at all. It had become a private matter for me, something no longer connected to writing. All the research for the biography, all the facts I would uncover as I dug into his past, all the work that seemed to belong to the book--these were the very things I would use to find out where he was (316).

His investigations lead him into his own and Fanshawe's childhood, into a sexual encounter with Fanshawe's mother after which he "wanted to kill Fanshawe" (315). His world becomes darker and darker as he enters his own past. "This was the tangible evidence, the remains of a dead world. I had stepped into the museum of my own past, and what I found there nearly crushed me" (303). The reason for his struggle is that in order to do his job properly, he must also look at himself and admit the superior position of Fanshawe, no matter to what extent. Fanshawe is the young, intelligent, independent boy with his own morals and standards, the young man who continued to refine his writing skills and the person who even in 'death' is the better and more successful writer. The narrator never had "such a book" (244), a good novel, inside him. "The world saw me as a bright young fellow, a new critic on the rise, but inside myself I felt old, already used up. What I had done so far amounted to a mere fraction of nothing at all. It was so much dust, and the slightest wind would blow it away" (245).

He abandons his life and family in New York to track Fanshawe first in America, then in Paris. A whole chapter is dedicated to the narrator's experience in this European metropolis that is so different from New York and America in general. "Things felt oddly bigger to me in Paris. The sky was more present than in New

York, its whims more fragile. (...) I felt as though I had been turned upside-down. This was an old world city (...). I had been displaced (...). I felt my grip loosening (...)" (338). The culture shock of the "old world" leads him into his deeply felt experience of 'postmodern' displacement. He has to give in to his own inability of finding Fanshawe since "there were no leads, no clues to follow. Fanshawe was buried somewhere, and his whole life was buried with him. Unless he wanted to be found, I didn't have a ghost of a chance" (340). In true 'Blue-fashion', he is not even able to call his wife and instead loses himself in "another world" (346) of prostitutes and drinking. As he fails to find Fanshawe, he settles for a scapegoat by the name of Stillman (!)--an unlucky patron who enters a Paris bar. "He's no one, I said to myself (...) and if he's no one, then he must be Fanshawe. (...) It made no sense, and because of that, it made all the sense in the world. (...) I was the sublime alchemist who would change the world at will" (348/351). Auster again dwells on the notion of chance and the arbitrariness of a fragmented world, in which the narrator's only hope is to kill an innocent 'somebody' to rid himself of Fanshawe's superiority. In the utterly grotesque scene that follows, he chases 'Fanshawe-Stillman' through Paris and they get into a fight that very much resembles Blue's and Black's fight in *Ghosts* or the final one in Poe's "William Wilson". He fails to kill him, is nearly killed himself and ends up lying half-dead in his hotel room for three days, almost unhappy not to have died. "It felt strange to be alive, almost incomprehensible. (...) The sensation of life had dribbled out of me (...), the undeniable odor of nothingness" (352) was rushing through his veins. He seems to have sought the same relief from the "nothingness" of his existence as Quinn in CoG. "I became inert, a thing that did not move, and little by little I lost track of myself" (345). In this case, however, the 'detective' felt that he must return to his home and family and abandon the fruitless search for Fanshawe. The narrator returns to New York, re-establishes a relationship with his wife and tries to lead a normal life. He stops writing the biography, hires an agent for Fanshawe's books and decides together with his wife never to talk about him again. However, deep inside he knew that there were still things to come. "I knew that the story wasn't over. My last month in Paris had taught me that, and little by little I learned to accept that. It was only a matter of time before the next thing happened" (355). So he waits for Fanshawe to make the next move and when Fanshawe asks him to come to Boston he goes, hoping that a confrontation will finally resolve his dilemma.

This leads us right to the end of the story and the aspect of closure. Several times in the novel we are confronted with the announcement of the narrator that "this is where the story should end" (278), that "this was the end of the line for [him]" (342), that "[he] was coming to an end now" (340), that he and his wife "are coming to the end" (337), only to go on by constantly reminding us that "it turns out that this is only the beginning" (278), that "the worst of it began now" (316), that he "knew that the story wasn't over" (355), and that "stories without endings can do nothing but go on forever" (278). "In the end" (317), this exactly summarises the whole aspect of closure in Auster's trilogy: "The end, however, is clear to me. I have not forgotten it. (...) The entire story comes down to what happened at the end, and without that end inside me now, I could not have started that book" (346).What really happened "when [he] is nearly at the end" (354)? He finds Fanshawe in Boston, but never gets to see him because Fanshawe hides in a 'locked room' and threatens to kill himself and the narrator if he tried to open the door. Fanshawe offers his former friend a red notebook (could that be the same one Quinn filled with his words?) in which he is supposed to find an explanation for his actions, to answer questions that had been left unanswered. But what he receives is more frustrating than illuminating:

> If I say nothing about what I found there, it is because I understood very little. All the words were familiar to me, and yet they seemed to have been put together strangely, as though their final purpose was to cancel each other out. (...) Each sentence erased the sentence before it, each paragraph made the next paragraph impossible. (...) It is as if Fanshawe knew his final work had to subvert any expectation I had for it. (...) He had answered the question by asking another question, and therefore everything remained open, unfinished, to be started again (370).

The reader is also left frustrated because the narrator does not even share the contents of the red notebook with him. The reader has encountered a plurality of worlds that goes along with a plurality of possible endings, in which Auster decides "to choose not to choose (...), because to let the mystery exist does not restrict his freedom to a single choice and, at the same time, potentially implies all solutions without choosing any."[109] "There were empty spaces for me, blanks in the picture, and no matter how successful I was in filling the other areas, doubts would remain, which meant that the

---

[109] Tani, p. 46.

work could never truly be finished" (344). The nameless narrator decides to destroy the red notebook page by page, freeing himself finally of the last remains of Fanshawe's existence. Neither he, nor the reader has solved the case and just as it has been the case with Quinn and Blue, we will never find out whether he will return to his family or disappear into the "nothingness" of the postmodern world(s). "I came to the last page just as the train was pulling *out* [my italics]" (371).

In Auster's *In The Country of Last Things*, Anna Blume admits that

> the closer you come to the end, the more there is to say. The end is only imaginary, a destination you invent to keep yourself going, but a point comes when you realize you will never get there. You might have to stop, but that is only because you have run out of time. You stop, but that does not mean you have come to the end.[110]

"That's what the story boils down to, I think. A series of lost chances. All the pieces were there from the beginning, but no one knew how to put them together."[111]

---

[110] Paul Auster, *In the Country of Last Things* (London: Faber and Faber, 1987), p. 183.
[111] Paul Auster, *Moon Palace* (New York: Penguin Books, 1989), p. 249.

Americans have no identity,
but they do have wonderful teeth.
--Jean Baudrillard--

4 The Quest for Identity: The Self and the Other, or Doubles and more Doubles

The remark by Jean Baudrillard in his latest work *America*[112] is, of course, supposed to evoke protest and reflection upon the notion of identity in America. It rather fits, however, into the discussion of Auster's treatment of identity in the NYT. Charles Baxter echoes this aspect when he notes that

> the achievement of Paul Auster's fiction (...) is to combine an American obsession with gaining an identity with the European ability to ask how, and under what conditions, identity is stolen or lost.(...) *The New York Trilogy* gives us a set of wondrous mazes of identity, peopled with mysterious observers, authorial surrogates, mirrors facing mirrors, and persons missing to one degree or another.[113]

In postmodern investigations of human subjectivities, the self can be split into many selves to explore the peculiarities of self. Postmodern literature in general frequently deals with the process of the individual becoming destabilised and fragmented.[114] Among others, Linda Hutcheon stresses the concept of the decentered subject[115] when she notes that

> the philosophical, 'archeological' and psychoanalytical de-centering of the concept of the subject has been led by Derrida, Foucault, Lacan, among others. To decenter is not

---

[112] Jean Baudrillard, *America* (London: Verso, 1989), p. 34.

[113] Charles Baxter, "The Bureau of Missing Persons: Notes on Paul Auster's Fiction", *Review of Contemporary Fiction* 14:1, 1994, pp. 41/2.

[114] cf. Ihab Hassan, *The Dismemberment of Orpheus, Toward a Postmodern Literature* (Madison: University of Wisconsin Press, 1982). I do not want to elaborate further on the discussion among postmodern critics whether the subject--decentered, alienated, fragmented or else--has been relinquished or totally obliterated in our postmodern time or whether it has always been a factor in the discussion. I refer the reader to the works of William Spanos (*Repetitions 4*), Hans Bertens ("The Postmodern *Weltanschauung* and its relation with Modernism: An Introductory Survey"), Ihab Hassan (who later pushes his thoughts about disappearing ontology much further in *Paracriticism* than in *The Dismemberment of Orpheus*), or Frederic Jameson, who states in "Postmodernism and Consumer Society" (in: Hal Foster (ed), *The Anti-Aesthetic: Essays on Postmodern Culture*, Seattle: Bay Press, 1983) that "individualism and personal identity is a fact of the past" (114). A fact is, that the subject, hence the individual and his identity, appears as a central aspect beyond the surface mystery of the detective stories in Auster's trilogy.

[115] Very generally, decentering means that a 'structure' in question is not organized around a fixed center (which could be a stable identity, reason or consciousness), but is rather a 'decentered entity'. This notion has been introduced by Freud and his theory of the 'Unconscious', which casts doubt on whether the rational, conscious mind could be regarded as center of subjectivity.

to deny, however. Postmodernism does not, as Terry Eagleton asserts, mistake 'the disintegration of certain traditional ideologies of the subject for the subject's final disappearance' [1985, 70]. Its historicising of the subject and of its customary (centering) anchors radically problematises the entire notion of subjectivity, pointing directly to its dramatised contradictions. (...) As Derrida insists: 'The subject is absolutely indispensable. I don't destroy the subject; I situate it.' (...) To situate is also to acknowledge the ideology of the subject and to suggest alternative notions of subjectivity.[116]

"Self-less-ness" (the loss of self and hence a de-centeredness) is also present in Ihab Hassan's catena of postmodern features, which is discussed in the chapter on postmodernism.

In CoG, G, and TLR we are confronted with a "well-choreographed dance of *doppelgängers*,"[117] "a meditation on the problematic of self-identity (...) and between signification and selfhood,"[118] 'decentered' writer-detectives on the search for meaning, truth, and a coherent world. Alison Russell confirms this aspect when she says that "confused identities, twins, doubles, and mirror images appear repeatedly in the trilogy."[119] In CoG, Quinn starts following Stillman but sees another person whose "face was the exact twin of Stillman's" (68); in G, Blue feels as though he were "looking into a mirror" (172) and the narrator of TLR reads one of Fanshawe's stories that deals with "the confused identities of two sets of twins" (253).

The detectives and searchers in Auster's fiction realise that possession of meaning invariably lies in becoming one with the 'Other', the object of their surveillance of search. The fact that significance in the world only emerges as the consequence of the relation between one's self and another motivates these characters, who suffer from their split self and are constantly looking for the 'Other' to find their own 'Self' in order to relieve them from their identity crises. These crises--often brought on by the unstable and chaotic culture which the subject finds itself in--affect the consciousness of the subject and its relationship with others. It does, however, always take a coincidence, a moment of pure chance, a rupture to shake the self from its apathy, from the pseudo-intimacy it maintains with itself: the wrong number in CoG, the strange case in G, or the sudden reappearance of

---

[116] Hutcheon, *A Poectis of Postmodernism*, p. 159.
[117] Bawer, p.69.
[118] Steven E. Alford, "Spaced-Out: Signification and Space in Paul Auster's *The New York Trilogy*", *Contemporary Literature* 36:4, 1995, p. 615.
[119] Alison Russell, "Deconstructing *The New York Trilogy*", p. 83.

Fanshawe into the life of the narrator. The binary oppositions and double relationships--a literary feature of Romanticism--between Quinn-Stillman, Blue-Black, and the narrator-Fanshawe are 'postmodernly' deconstructed and subverted since Auster links characters and texts invariably. References to Quinn, Stillman, and Henry Dark reappear in TLR. In CoG, Quinn is equally 'attracted' to both Stillmans and Auster, the character.

According to Jacques Lacan, the 'Other' is everything the subject is not (anyone who is not 'I'), as well as everything the subject does not have. Additionally, as all individuals are constructed through the acquisition of the power to express desires and needs through language, the 'Other' actually defines the 'Self' because it is the ultimate signifier of everything I am not.[120] In Lacan's concept of the 'Mirror Stage', the 'imaginary self' is formed in a moment of 'misrecognition'. A person (mostly a child) who sees 'itself' in the mirror forms an 'imaginary self', in which the observer and its reflection are not distinct anymore. Thus, a person's conception of itself is fundamentally based on a fiction.[121] This notion is transposed by Auster in the various doublings and 'fictionalisations' of the characters in the NYT. In "Why Write?" Auster precisely illustrates that motivation of placing identity in the center of his work, when he admits that "every time I saw my face in the mirror, I seemed to be looking at someone else." [122] In *The Art of Hunger* he provides us with further information on his own perception and treatment of identity in the trilogy. He wants to reveal the problems that go along with different identities, and raise

> the question of who is who and whether or not we are who we think we are. The whole process that Quinn undergoes in that book--and the characters in the other two, as well-- is one of stripping away to some barer condition in which we have to face up to who we are. Or who we aren't. It finally comes down to the same thing. (...) The detective really is a very compelling figure, a figure we all understand. He's the seeker after truth, the problem solver, the one who tries to figure things out. But what if, in the course of trying to figure it out, you just unveil more mysteries? I suppose maybe that's what happens in the books.[123]

---

[120] cf. Jacques Lacan, "The Subject and the Other: Alienation", in: Jacques-Alain Miller, *Four Fundamental Concepts* (New York: Norton, 1978).
[121] cf. Jacques Lacan, "The Mirror Stage as Formative of the Function of the 'I' as Revealed in Psychoanalytic Experience", in: Lacan, *Ecrits: A Selection* (New York: Norton, 1977). Lacan's thesis, which stresses that the subject is constituted in and by its language is also of importance for the trilogy, as we will see in the chapter on language.
[122] Paul Auster, "Why Write?", *The New Yorker* 71:42, Dec.25, 1995 & Jan.1, 1996, p.86.
[123] Auster, *The Art of Hunger*, p. 262.

Apparently, he does not seek what separates people, but, rather, what brings them together; namely a similar confusion about their identity. Pascal Bruckner claims that Paul Auster is a "detective of the self." He applies an "uncompromising narrative skill to a metaphysical quest: why is there a self rather than nothing? To faciliate this task, he presents his fiction in the protective guise of the detective novel."[124] Considering these points, this paper closely examines the notion of identity in the NYT. As this notion is most prominent in CoG, more consideration is given to this novel than to G and TLR.

4.1 Quinn

In CoG, it is already the first sentence that should strike the attentive reader as a 'prognosis' of the whole book: "It was a wrong number that started it, the telephone ringing three times in the dead of the night, and the voice on the other end asking for *someone he was not*" (3) [my italics]. "Placed from 'the other end'--or the Other's end--the wrong number, or errant call, appears by chance, the result perhaps of crossed lines, and arrives at the protagonist's place only to dis-place him, only to mis-take him for an other."[125] In the whole novel, the writer-detective Quinn constantly appears as a character who is taking on multiple identities and pretending to be someone "he is not."

Even though "there is little that need detain us" (3) about Quinn, we are told at the very beginning that he writes mystery novels under the "name of William Wilson" (3) (a *doppelgänger* short story by Poe), a pseudonym Quinn has taken on after the death of his wife and son, since he "was no longer that part of him that could write books, and although in many ways Quinn continued to exist, he no longer existed for anyone but himself" (5). Quinn continues to write but switches from poetry, essays and plays to mystery novels, which enable him to live under another identity, because "he did not consider himself to be the author of what he wrote (...). William Wilson, after all, was an invention, and even though he had been born

[124] Pascal Bruckner, "Paul Auster, or The Heir Intestate", in: Dennis Barone, *Beyond the Red Notebook*, p. 32.
[125] William G. Little, "Nothing to Go On: Paul Auster's *City of Glass*", *Contemporary Literature* 38:1, 1997, p. 152.

within Quinn himself, he now lived an independent life. (...) He and William Wilson [never] were the same man" (5). Auster, however, takes the binary opposition of the 'W' (double-you) a step further and places Quinn within a triad formation of identities: Quinn lives simultaneously through his novels' hero, the detective Max Work (quite a telling-name here!), with which he feels a strong bondage:

> Over the years, Work had become very close to Quinn. Whereas William Wilson remained an abstract figure for him, Work had increasingly come to life. In the triad of selves that Quinn had become, Wilson served as a kind of ventriloquist, Quinn himself was the dummy, and Work was the animated voice that gave purpose to the enterprise. If Wilson was an illusion, he nevertheless justified the lives of the other two. If Wilson did not exist, he nevertheless was the bridge that allowed Quinn to pass from himself into Work. And little by little, Work had become a presence in Quinn's life, his interior brother, his comrade in solitude (6-7).

Barry Lewis notes, that in Auster's "probings into the frailties of human identity, (...) the breakdown of the detection process is always accompanied by a breakdown of the self."[126] In this sense, Auster's novels (CoG as much as the other two) would fit into Tani's category of the "deconstructive anti-detective novel", in which

> reality is so tentacular and full of clues that the detective risks his sanity as he tries to find a solution. In a very Poesque way, the confrontation is no longer between a detective and a murderer, but between the detective and reality, or between the detective's mind and his sense of identity, which is falling apart, between the detective and the 'murderer' in his own self.[127]

Detection is more a quest for identity as the unveiling of a crime. The mystery outside releases the mystery inside the detective. The detective's self becomes unstable and inconsistent. Therefore, one might be tempted to argue, Quinn, the detective in CoG, lives in a triad of selves that has enabled him so far to live within a comparatively stable self. Wilson does not disturb the closeness between Quinn and Work, the second self, which is more real than its author: "(...) Work continued to live in the world of others, and the more Quinn seemed to vanish, the more persistent Work's presence in that world became" (10). Through Wilson and Work, Quinn fictionalises himself twice, thus achieving to be at the center of things by entering his own novels and Work's identity, his second self. "Whereas Quinn tended to feel out of place in his own skin, Work was aggressive, quick-tongued, at home in whatever spot he happened to find himself. The very things that caused problems for Quinn,

---

[126] Lewis, p. 60.
[127] Tani, p. 76.

Work took for granted, and he walked through the mayhem of his adventures with an ease and indifference that never failed to impress his creator" (10). As he enters his own fiction, "he had, of course, long ago stopped thinking of himself as real. If he lived now in the world at all, it was only at one remove, through the imaginary person of Max Work. His detective necessarily had to be real" (10). In this context, Carin Freywald comments that one of the "basic convictions in the trilogy [is] that fiction is more real than fact, for Quinn (...) is an invention of himself."[128] Quinn's fictitious triad of selves is also mirrored in his perception of the detective, the private eye.

> The term held a triple meaning for Quinn. Not only was it the letter 'i', standing for 'investigator', it was 'I' in the upper case, the tiny life-bud buried in the body of the breathing self. At the same time, it was also the physical eye of the writer, the eye of the man who looks out from himself into the world and demands that the world reveal itself to him. For five years now [the period after the death of his family], Quinn had been living in the grip of this pun (9/10).

Becoming a private eye enables him to submerge his private 'I', to depersonalise himself, in just the same way that his rambles around New York reduce him to a 'seeing eye'.

> New York was an inexhaustible space, a labyrinth of endless steps, and no matter how far he walked, no matter how well he came to know its neighborhoods and streets, it always left him with the feeling of being lost. Lost not only in the city, but within himself as well. Each time he took a walk, he felt as though he were leaving himself behind, and by giving himself up to the movement of the streets, by reducing himself to a seeing eye, he was able to escape the obligation to think, and this, more than anything else, brought him a measure of peace, a salutary emptiness within. The world was outside him, around him (...). On his best walks, he was able to feel that he was nowhere. And this, finally, was all he ever asked of things: to be nowhere (4).

A little bit later in the novel we learn more about Quinn's walks and their significance, concerning his identity and the inner and outer world:

> Quinn was used to wandering. His excursions through the city had taught him to understand the connectedness of inner and outer. (...) On his best days he could bring the outside in and thus usurp the sovereignty of inwardness. By flooding himself with externals, by drowning himself out of himself, he had managed to exert some small degree of control over his fits of despair. Wandering, therefore, was a kind of mindlessness (74).

For him, New York, "the nowhere he had built around him " (4), his surroundings, and his own personality 'Quinn', constitute the outer world as opposed to his inner

---

[128] Carin Freywald, "How Philip Marlowe came to New York City", p. 148.

world which alternates between his second self, Work, and a "mindlessness," a void, a nothingness. In the turmoil of so many identities and problems, he seeks an inner state of mind that projects him into a sort of 'Neverland' (which is also the title of Fanshawe's first novel in TLR), a country of nothingness. Anne Holzapfel supports this argument when she maintains that "by blending inner and outer Quinn manages to separate himself from his self, while simultaneously being able to control it."[129]

What adds to the reader's confusion even more (after such a bombardment of names, puns, identities, and 'real' fictions) is Quinn's adoption of another identity, the detective Paul Auster. The character Auster, and thus Quinn's new identity, are born on "May nineteenth" (11), the day when Quinn was conceived by his parents, and which he secretly celebrates as his birthday. It is the exact same date, when Quinn receives the third phone call and says: "This is Auster speaking. (...) He paused for a moment to let the words sink in, as much as for himself as for the other" (12). This marks the beginning of the case for Quinn, alias, Wilson, alias Work, alias the detective Paul Auster. The 'Other' will be Stillman. Or both, Senior and Junior. Or Auster? Or the reader?

Quinn begins to like his new identity, which at the same time doubles him once more. "The effect of being Paul Auster was not altogether unpleasant. (...) He felt as though he had somehow been taken out of himself, as if he no longer walked around with the burden of his own consciousness" (61). Through Auster's identity, Quinn finally achieves what he has been looking for on his endless walks through New York: To be nowhere, to bury himself in the indeterminacy and fragmentation of the postmodern world. "To be Auster meant being a man with no interior, a man with no thoughts. And if there were no thoughts available to him, if his inner life had been made inaccessible, then there was no place for him to retreat to" (75). However, as it turns out, being Paul Auster is not as easy and uncomplicated as Quinn had thought it would be, knowing that "it was all an illusion" (62). Arthur Saltzman writes that "what had begun as a vacation from self-consciousness and inanition for Quinn (the adoption of the Auster persona) becomes a full-blown identity crisis."[130] The constant shifts and changes in Quinn's personality as he follows Stillman's

---

[129] Holzapfel, p. 34.
[130] Arthur Saltzman, *Designs of Darkness in Contemporary American Fiction* (Philadelphia: University of Pennsylvania Press, 1990), p. 60.

traces, draw him deeper and deeper into the abyss of his own 'self-less-ness.' When he takes on the case, Quinn doubts the 'reality' of his existence, of the case, of the world. Like a puppet that is led by the 'authorial' master, he only *seems* to be doing things. "I seem to be going out. (...) I seem to have arrived. (...) Even that locution, *his appointment*, seemed odd to him. It wasn't his appointment, it was Paul Auster's. And who that person was he had no idea" (14/15).

The appointment with Peter Stillman Jr. (who happens to have the same first name as Quinn's dead son) confronts Quinn with another character that suffers from an identity problem, caused by the cruelty of his father's experiments. "I am Peter Stillman. (...) That is not my real name" (18). And a little later the 'still man' adds: "For now, I am still Peter Stillman. That is not my real name. I cannot say who I will be tomorrow. Each day is new, and each day I am born again" (26). Somehow, Stillman seems to have sensed some traces of a split personality in Quinn as well when he asks him: "What is your name Mr Auster? Perhaps you are the real Mr Sad, and I am no one" (20). Quinn echoes this in his entry into the red notebook. "Listen to me. My name is Paul Auster. That is not my real name" (49). What is Quinn's real name then? The ones he has chosen for himself, Wilson and Work, only lead him into the realms of fiction. The one that has been given to him by mere coincidence, Auster, does not seem to help him either as he is confronted with the 'real' Auster in the novel, who resembles in many aspects the man Quinn used to be in his "other life" (39). In *Lost in the Funhouse*, John Barth dwells on the same notion of the arbitrariness and fragmentation of the self. "Among other things I haven't a proper name. The one I bear's misleading, if not false. I didn't choose it either."[131] Quinn is somehow overwhelmed with pity and sympathy for Peter, feeling the obligation to save him. "He knew he could not bring his own son back to life, but at least he could prevent another one from dying" (41). Stillman considers him "the answer" (38) to his fears and doubts, but Quinn is not a stable character, a man in the center of things but is rather very unsure of his own place in the world.

Quinn's insecurity continues when he starts following Stillman Sr. As Quinn notices by simply observing Stillman, that he is not going to get useful results in this investigation of "two twins cleaving together" (52), he decides to talk to him

---

[131] John Barth, *Lost in the Funhouse* (London: Secker and Warburg, 1969), p.35.

personally. "He had lived Stillman's life, walked at his pace, seen what he had seen, and the only thing he felt now was the man's impenetrability. Instead of narrowing the distance that lay between him and Stillman, he had seen the old man slip away from him, even as he remained before his eyes" (80). This is the point in the story when the confusion, the doubling of names and the 'pushing around' of multiple identities becomes an endless game, "where the detective gets lost" (65).

In the first of his meetings with Stillman, Quinn introduces himself saying: "My name is Quinn" (88). Actually, he is supposed to be Auster, and thus Quinn serves as a pseudonym. Stillman, intuitively grasping Quinn's multiple identities, replies: "I like your name enormously, Mr Quinn: It flies off in so many little directions at once" (90). Quinn, aware of this fact, confirms Stillman's foreseeing: "Yes, I often noticed that myself" (90). During the second encounter, Quinn pretends to be Henry Dark, a fictitious person, Stillman has invented for his dissertation *The Garden and the Tower: Early Visions of the New World*. Therefore, Stillman doubts Quinn's existence as Henry Dark, but Quinn, fictionalising himself again, insists on the true nature of his existence: "Well, perhaps I'm another Henry Dark. As opposed to the one who doesn't exist" (96). In their final meeting, Quinn takes on the name Peter Stillman, a name, as we are all aware of, that is held by the son and the father. Here, Auster, creates another triplet of identites. "'My name is Peter Stillman,' said Quinn. 'That's my name,' answered Stillman. 'I'm Peter Stillman.' 'I'm the other Peter Stillman,' said Quinn. 'Oh. You mean my son. Yes, that's possible. You just look like him'" (101). Stillman concisely expresses what the whole book with regard to identity seems to bring across. "One minute we're one thing, and then another" (101). Quinn, trying to save the son from whatever evil the father may harbor, adopts the role of the lost son, seeking knowledge from the father. "A father must always teach his son the lessons he has learned. In that way knowledge is passed down from generation to generation, and we grow wise" (103). (...) 'You mustn't forget anything', he tells Quinn, who replies, 'I won't, father. I promise'" (104).[132] Quinn's

---

[132] The relationship father/son is a constant feature in Auster's work. Due to restrictions of space, I do not want to further elaborate on that aspect in this paper but rather refer the reader to Joshua Kendall's essay, "Psychische Zersplitterung in der postmodernen Polis: Kaspar Hauser in Paul Auster's *New York Trilogy*", in: Ulrich Struve (ed.), *Der imaginierte Findling. Studien zur Kaspar-Hauser-Rezeption* (Heidelberg: Universitätsverlag, 1995), p. 207-222 and Arthur Saltzman's book, *Designs of Darkness in Contemporary American Fiction*.

search for Stillman is mainly a search for himself, another dispossessed father of a boy named Peter.

But again, Quinn is not able to gain any coherent information or clues about Stillman's behavior and his further proceedings, apart from a few more details about his crazy language theories. Matching his routines, notetaking habits, and totally adapting to his behavior, Quinn finds himself becoming indistinguishable from his subject. He desperately clings to the case, the one thing that nourishes his existence, even though Virginia Stillman explains to him that "no one can watch a person twenty-four hours a day. (...) You'd have to be inside his skin." Quinn reveals his inner turmoil to her by replying: "'That's just the trouble. I thought I was'" (108). He has lost track of Stillman who suddenly vanished in the middle of the night, and this is when his crisis reaches its climax. He locates the 'real' Paul Auster, the man whom he has been masquerading as, but Auster is no detective either, just a writer like Quinn. He is of no further help to him, but rather intensifies his irritation. Auster and his family, his wife Siri (Paul Auster's real wife), and his son Daniel (of course, Quinn and the young Auster share the same first name: "'Daniel, this is Daniel'" [122], says Auster) impersonate everything he had lost years ago: the stable existence, domestic serenity, love, and warmth of a family, it was worth living for. "[Quinn] felt as though Auster were taunting him with the things he had lost" (121). "(...) He responded with envy and rage, a lacerating self-pity" (121), since Quinn would have liked to 'be' Auster, to lead his life. "Quinn felt a little more of himself collapse" (122), as the world around him becomes an indistinguishable place of multiple personalities. "Everybody's Daniel. (...) I'm you, and you're me. And around and around it goes" (122). Quinn has met and lost another of his selves at the same time. Quinn's "Good-bye myself" (122) is the starting point of Quinn's final disappearing. Even though "Quinn was nowhere now" (124), a place he has longed to be at so insistently, he "was now before the beginning, and so far before the beginning that it was worse than any end he could imagine" (124). Ultimately, Quinn resigns himself to a life in waiting, spying for months from the alley on his clients, which results in losing himself so completely that he barely feels the loss:

> Now, as he looked at himself in the shop mirror, he was neither shocked nor disappointed. (...) Yes, it seemed more than likely that this was Quinn. Even now, however, he was not upset. The transformation in his appearance had been so drastic that he could not help but be fascinated by it. He had turned into a bum. (...) It did not

really matter. He had been one thing before, and now he was another. It was neither better nor worse. It was different and that was all (142/43).

However, it is not only different, it is also the end for Quinn who, due to his innumeral identities, slowly disappears into nothingness. Dennis Barone states that "Quinn empties himself; literally, he thins away to disappearance."[133] "[His apartment] was gone, he was gone, everything was gone" (150). There is, however, one more identity left for him to retreat into: Peter Stillman Jr.'s identity as a child, lying naked in a room, alone, isolated, barely aware of his own existence. Quinn reduces himself to the writer he was before the case, dedicates his time to filling the red notebook with words "that had nothing to do with the Stillman case" (128). "For the case was far behind him now, and he no longer bothered to think about it. It had been a bridge to another place in his life, and now that he had crossed it, its meaning had been lost" (156). In the same way as the identity of the "two Wilson's cancelled each other out" (153), Quinn cancels his own identities. The notebook becomes more and more the center of Quinn's thoughts which evolve around the notion of disappearance. As the last page of the notebook is filled, Quinn disappears, his identities "flying off in all directions" (90). Quinn has been the victim of his own decentralisation, fragmentation and fictionalisation. His own lack of introspection, his willingness to inhabit the self of others, his desire to lose his self in the streets of New York adequately accounts for a figure that has not succeeded in finding his place in the world, neither here nor there. During his quest for identity, coherence, and a centered existence, becoming Max Work did not 'work out' for him, neither did trying to impersonate Paul Auster, Stillman, Henry Dark, or the two William Wilsons. As we are left behind without an answer to the question of Quinn's real identity, we learn that--as it is with the concept of a good detective novel, according to Quinn--"the center, then, is everywhere, and no circumference can be drawn until the book has come to an end" (9). Unfortunately, or maybe fortunately, the book never comes to an end.

---

[133] Dennis Barone, "Auster's Memory", *Review of Contemporary Fiction* 14:1, 1994, p. 34.

4.2 Blue

In G, multiple identities and the corresponding problems that arise with a loss of self
are not as obviously interwoven into the story as they have been in CoG. On the
surface, Blue is presented as a "solid character on the whole, less given to dark
thoughts than most" (187). He is hired to spy on Black, a case which demands that he
move into a one-room apartment in Brooklyn, say good-bye to his fiancée--"don't
worry, if I'm out of touch for a while" (163)--and totally rely on himself for quite a
while, something he is not used to. "He has moved rapidly along the surface of things
for as long as he can remember, fixing his attention on these surfaces only in order to
perceive them, sizing up one and then passing on to the next, and he has always taken
pleasure in the world as such, asking no more of things than that they be there" (171).
So far, Blue's life and his existence have taken place on the surface, on the outer side
of his self. He has been taking almost everything for granted and is not yet prepared
for the journey *into* the self, which he experiences in the novel. Martin Klepper
underlines this issue when he writes that

> Die Suche nach dem Anderen draußen (sei es Täter oder Opfer, Vater, Bruder,
> Liebhaber oder Freund) ist dabei immer gleichzeitig eine Reise ins Innere, eine Suche
> nach der eigenen Identität, angedeutet durch die quintessentielle Doppelgänger-
> Beziehung, in der bei Auster alle Suchenden zu den Gesuchten stehen.[134]

Due to the anonymous nature of the case, in which he is only allowed to keep a
written contact in form of weekly reports to his client and in which he concentrates
solely on Black, he is isolated from the outer world. What else is left for him than to
turn inward into his own self?

> For the first time in his life, he finds that he has been thrown back on himself, with
> nothing to grab hold of, nothing to distinguish one moment from the next. He has never
> given much thought to the world inside him, and though he always knew it was there, it
> has remained an unknown quantity, unexplored and therefore dark, even to himself
> (171).

---

[134] Klepper, p. 251. (The quest for the Other always goes hand in hand with a journey into the self, a
quest for one's own identity, which is present in Auster's work through the quintessential interrelationship of doubles; an interrelationship, in which the seekers are side by side with the ones that
are being sought after [my translation].

He is forced to scrutinise his own darkness during the long hours of his observing Black. A process that makes him experience features of himself, that, until now, he has not been familiar with. "Life has slowed down so drastically for him that Blue is now able to see things that have previously escaped his attention. (...) The beating of his heart, the sound of his breath, the blinking of his eyes--Blue is now aware of these tiny events, and try as he might to ignore them, they persist in his mind like a nonsensical phrase repeated over and over again" (172). He feels trapped by the case, by Black, by the book--*Walden*--he is reading and does not understand. He questions the coherent meaning of his existence, of his life and of the case. "Blue has been groping about in the darkness, feeling blindly for the light switch, a prisoner of the case itself. (...) They have trapped Blue into doing nothing, into being so inactive as to reduce his life to almost no life at all. Yes, says Blue to himself, that's what it feels like: like nothing at all" (201). Unlike Quinn in CoG, Blue does not strive for a state of 'nothingness' but rather resents it. He does, however, like Quinn, turn to his double, hoping for an answer to his inner struggles and at the same time trying to do the necessary detective work. "The only way for Blue to have a sense of what is happening is to be inside Black's mind, to see what he is thinking (...)" (166). Slowly, he feels that his personality is taking on a different course. "I'm changing, he says to himself. Little by little, I'm no longer the same" (174). Having met an almost impenetrable net of doubles and pseudonyms in CoG, the reader in G is only faced with a single pair, which has been established as a stable presence from the very beginning of the novel. We encounter Blue's doubling through his opponent Black, and not, as in CoG, by means of pseudonyms and endless fictionalisations. Auster seems to complete what he has prepared in CoG through his making use of Poe's "William Wilson": a detective story on the surface, building the ground for a Poesque *doppelgänger* story presented in a postmodern fashion. Little hints that aim to open the reader's eyes for the rather obvious relation are scattered throughout the text. "Blue estimates Black's age to be the same as his, give or take a year or two" (165/66). Slowly, Blue develops a certain awareness of his developing interrelationship with Black, "for in spying out at Black across the street, it is as though Blue were looking into a mirror, and instead of merely watching another, he finds that he is also watching himself" (172). This mirror image is reflected in a story in one of the endless magazines Blue has been reading (this one is actually quite telling again, called *Stranger than Fiction*!). We are told about a young man, who goes skiing and happens to hit upon the same spot where his father had been swallowed up by an avalanche. He detects a perfectly intact body, preserved by the ice, and stops to examine it. "(...) He bent down and looked at the face of the corpse (...) looking at himself. (...) He saw that it was his father" (179/80). When Alison Russell describes "*Ghosts* as a self-enclosed structure of self-mirrorings"[135], one is tempted to add that G is a story of 'meta-self-mirrorings', mirrorings about mirrorings.

Only much later does Blue find out that he is being watched as well and that his life reflects the one Thoreau describes in *Walden*, the book Black is reading (A book published by "Walter J. Black" [181]), and which is at the same time the source for the story-within-the story of *Ghosts*. Black records everything Blue has been doing and vice versa. "To speculate, from the Latin speculatus, meaning to spy out, to observe, and linked to the word speculum, meaning mirror or looking glass" (171/72). The 'City of Glass', a transparent world, perpetually copying itself through the actions of the protagonists, is transferred to Brooklyn, in which the 'ghosts' of Hawthorne's "Wakefield", Whitman's *Leaves of Grass* and Thoreau's *Walden* are hovering in the air. The roles of Black, who we suspect to be identical with White,[136] and Blue seem to be interchangeable, the observer and the observed, the detective and the 'detected'. "(...) If White is really out to get Blue and not Black, then perhaps Black has nothing to do with it, perhaps he is no more than an innocent bystander. In that case, it is Black who occupies the position Blue has assumed all along to be his, and Blue who takes the role of Black" (201). From the twinning of White and Black, Blue has uncovered a triad, one beyond his control.

---

[135] Russell, p. 77.

[136] Auster never explicitly reveals White's identity, but several clues in the text point to the assumption that they constitute the same person. When White comes into Blue's office, "it's impossible for Blue not to notice certain things about White (...). Blue is no amateur in the art of disguise" (135). Later, when Blue follows Black into the bookshop, Blue senses a certain similarity between Black and White, triggered by "the little glances he takes when Black seems not to be looking, [this] give[s] him the feeling that he has seen Black before, but he can't remember where" (181). Moreover, when Blue enters Black's apartment in the final climax scene, Black wears the same mask that the person we assume to be White was wearing when Blue tried to confront him in the post office where he picked up Blue's reports. "Black is wearing the mask again, the same one Blue saw on the man in the post office" (228).

Blue's identity is shaken to the grounds, he is torn between closeness and distance to Black. "There are moments when he feels so completely in harmony with Black, so naturally at one with the other man, that to anticipate what Black is going to do, to know when he will stay in his room and when he will go out, he need merely look into himself" (186). However, sometimes "there are times when he feels totally removed from Black, cut off from him in a way that is so stark and absolute that he begins to lose the sense of who he is" (186). Black feels the same way, they need one another to exist and to live independently from each other, a paradox Blue is conscious of.

> (...) He discovers the inherent paradox of his situation. For the closer he feels to Black, the less he finds it necessary to think about him. In other words, the more deeply entangled he becomes, the freer he is. What bogs him down is not involvement but separation. For it is only when Black seems to drift away from him that he must go out looking for him, and this takes time and effort, not to speak of struggle. At those moments when he feels closest to Black, however, he can begin to lead the semblance of an independent life (188).

This holds true for Black as well who reveals himself to Blue in a bar, perfectly knowing that Blue knows who he is and vice versa: "I've been watching him for so long now that I know him better than I know myself. All I have to do is think about him, and I know what he's doing, I know where he is, I know everything. It's come to the point that I can watch him with my eyes closed" (188). The difference between the two is, however, that Black knows from the beginning that he is being watched, since he, alias White has hired Blue to watch him, to write down his own life, minute for minute. Black, pretending to be a detective (and thus taking over Blue's role) in one of the encounters with Blue gives an answer to Blue's question whether his observed subject knew he was being observed: "Of course he knows. That's the whole point, isn't it? He's got to know, or else nothing makes sense. (...) Because he needs me, (...). He needs my eyes looking at him. He needs me to prove that he's alive" (216). For Blue, on the other hand, it takes longer to understand. "It seems perfectly plausible to him that he is also being watched, observed by another in the same way that he has been observing Black. If that is the case, then he has never been free. From the very beginning he has been the man in the middle, thwarted in front and hemmed in on the rear" (200).

To free himself from this dilemma, he has only one choice left: to kill his double, to kill the Other in order to free his Self. "If he doesn't take care of Black now, there will never be any end to it" (222). It has gone so far with Blue that "[he] can't breathe anymore. This is the end. I'm dying" (203). He is haunted by Black, "for no sooner does he begin to walk through these woods [the woods at Walden Pond?] (...) than he feels that Black is there, too, hiding behind some tree, (...), waiting for Blue to lie down and close his eyes before sneaking up on him and slitting his throat" (222). Charles Baxter points out that "to have a double, to see yourself mirrored in a twin, is the beginning of the feeling that something private and essential about you is being removed in a secretive and unpleasant way."[137] The final encounter and the fight between Black and Blue has been carefully prepared for by little hints in the text. Blue, for instance, says that "every man has his double somewhere. I don't see why mine can't be a dead man" (205). Black adds that "there are days when I don't know if I'll live that long. (...) One day we're alive, and the next day we're dead" (220/1). Blue enters Black's apartment, "blacks out" (223), overwhelmed by the fact that all the reports he had sent to White are "stacked neatly at the edge of Black's desk" (224). Steven Alford points out that "Blue's selfhood emerges as his Self in his 'reports'. But the reports themselves are not a discrete product of an autonomous, isolated self; they emerge as even feasible only through the possibility of the other's existence."[138] The narrator informs us that "it is not certain that Blue really recovers from the events of this night. And even if he does, it must be noted that several days go by before he returns to a semblance of his former self" (224). It is, however, highly questionable whether Blue really wants to return to his former self. Despite the terror, the isolation and the grief that Black has brought into Blue's life, he has shown him a way into his own self, into a better understanding of what he is, or not is. However, in true Poesque fashion, there can only survive one part of the double, the 'Other' will have to be a dead man. The double has to be split, since Blue knows that "to enter Black (...) was the equivalent of entering himself, and once inside himself, he can no longer conceive of being anywhere else" (226). He wants to "erase

---

[137] Charles Baxter, "The Bureau of Missing Persons: Notes on Paul Auster's Fiction", *Review of Contemporary Fiction* 14:1, 1994, p. 40.
[138] Steven E. Alford, "Mirror's of Madness: Paul Auster's *New York Trilogy*", *Critique* 37:1, 1995, p. 25.

the whole story", he "can no longer accept Black's existence, and therefore he denies it" (226) and confronts Black, who is armed with a gun, awaiting Blue. As in CoG, the 'whodunnit' finally gives way to a 'who-am-I'. The dramatic fight between Blue and Black is a replica of the final scene in Poe's "William Wilson", including the symbolic mask and the whisper.

> It was Wilson; but he no longer spoke in a whisper, and I could have fancied that I myself was speaking while he said: 'You have conquered and I yield. Yet henceforward art thou also dead--dead to the World, to heaven, and to hope! In me didst thou exist-- and, in my death, see by this image, which is thine own, how utterly thou hast murdered thyself.[139]
>
> [...]
>
> I always knew you were the right one for me. A man after my heart. (...) You were the whole world to me, Blue, and I turned you into my death. You're the one thing that doesn't change, the one thing that turns everything inside out. (...) It's going to be the two of us [dying] together, just like always (229/30).

As Blue wants to hear a solution to the 'case', a reason for his 'being involved' in this perverse game of the splitting of identities, a stop to the "doubletalk" (229), Black explains to him that "I've needed you from the beginning. If it hadn't been for you, I couldn't have done it. (...) Every time I looked up, you were there, watching me, following me, always in sight, boring into me with your eyes" (230). Auster seems to have come up with an explanation, at least one for Black's behavior and the 'case'. But what about Blue? We presume Black to be dead, although Blue "cannot say for certain whether Black is alive or dead" (231). He is not sure if the breathing is "coming from Black or himself" (231). Will Blue return to his former self? Will he now be able to live his life independently from Black? Has he learned to scrutinise his own self without losing it again, without getting lost in a world of 'glassy doubles'? As we are told by the narrator, and as it has been with Quinn in CoG, "from this moment, we know nothing" (232) about his future identity.

4.3 The Nameless Narrator

Usually, a trilogy is a work of art, which comprises three different yet corresponding parts, that are related to each other by a common theme (of course, a trilogy is not

---

[139] Edgar Allan Poe, "William Wilson", in: *The Fall of the House of Usher and Other Writings*, ed. David Galloway (London: Penguin, 1986), p. 178.

restricted to written work). The reader of a trilogy expects a coherent and final closure, as well as adequate answers to his questions, and this even more in a trilogy of detective novels. As we have learned earlier, Paul Auster is not willing to fulfill this 'normative request' of the reader. TLR rather seems to be a repetition of the preceding novels, especially when it comes to the nameless narrator's identity. In CoG, Quinn stands out as a character with a split identity right from the beginning; in G, Blue is presented as a stable character who, due to his case, is forced to scrutinise his own self only to lose it along the way; and in TLR, the nameless narrator has struggled to preserve a certain unity without the presence of his childhood companion Fanshawe. "He was the one who was with me, the one who shared my thoughts, the one I saw whenever I looked up from myself" (235). He has found a way to live independently from his constant shadow and double Fanshawe--Arthur Saltzman refers to Fanshawe and the narrator as "one another's twin ghosts"[140]--to break free from his influence to be able to exist within a centered selfness. "The fact was that I had let go of Fanshawe. His life had stopped the moment we went our separate ways, and he belonged to the past for me now, not to the present" (236). Yet, on a hardly perceptible, unconscious level, Fanshawe is still part of the narrator's existence. "He was a ghost I carried around inside me, a prehistoric figment, a thing that was no longer real" (236). He is still alive in the narrator's memory and in his thoughts: "By definition, a thought is something you are aware of. The fact that I did not once stop thinking about Fanshawe, that he was inside me day and night (...) was unknown to me at the time" (286). Although absent, Fanshawe still commands a presence, inherent within his writings and within the narrator's thoughts, for whom this quest is a "cause, a thing that justified me and made me feel important, and the more fully I disappeared into my ambitions for Fanshawe, the more sharply I came into focus for myself" (301). The ambivalence of a close contact and the loss of the 'Other' that results from this contact are constituted in the narrator's condition of his self-less-ness. "[Fanshawe] is the place where everything begins for me, and without him I would hardly know who I am. Whenever I think of my childhood now, I see Fanshawe" (235). Yet,

> I would get so close to him, would admire him so intensely, would want so desperately
> to measure up to him--and then suddenly a moment would come when I realised that he

---

[140] Saltzman, p. 67.

was alien to me, that the way he lived inside himself could never correspond to the way I needed to live. I wanted too much of things, I had too many desires, I lived too fully in the grip of the immediate ever to attain such indifference (251).

With the unexpected return of Fanshawe into his life, the narrator is thrown back into his past, into his memories, into his struggle. "Out of nowhere, Fanshawe had suddenly reappeared in my life. But no sooner was his name mentioned than he had vanished again" (236).

According to Klepper, Fanshawe's completeness and centeredness is openly described in logocentric terms.[141] He is "a sharply defined presence, (...) visible, whereas the rest of us were creatures without shape" (248), "always standing at the exact center of things" (255). This is also reflected in the quality of his character, in his "goodness" (251), and in his ability to "enter the feelings of another" (250). Even in their early childhood, the idealised Fanshawe possessed what the narrator still hopes for in vain, namely "that he was more truly himself than I could ever hope to be" (247).

There are, however, two sides to every story, and Fanshawe is no exception. His ideal and sharply defined presence, his 'centered normality' is repeatedly divided and split by his incompetence to exist side by side with others. Anne Holzapfel writes that "this circumstance [the other side of Fanshawe] is due to the fact that he has a talent to lose himself completely in others. It makes his life unbearable as he constantly alternates between the absolute self (...) and the self of others."[142] He is "detached" (251), "indifferent, (...) inaccessible" (248), "his dramas were of a different order" (249) and he frequently attempts to retreat into his own self, a "mysterious center of hiddenness" (248), something you cannot penetrate. For Fanshawe, the only possibility to exist is to be radically isolated from the Other. In his childhood, this is reflected in his cardboard "box, (...), his secret place", in which he "could go wherever he wanted to go, [he] could be wherever he wanted to be. But if another person ever entered his box, then its magic would be lost for good" (260). Later, Fanshawe abandons his wife and unborn child, avoiding any social contact, trying to lose himself in endless journeys, innumeral places, and anonymous jobs.

---

[141] cf. Klepper, p. 279.
[142] Holzapfel, p. 92.

The nameless narrator cannot cope with Fanshawe's sudden reappearance, with the memories he holds within himself. "I had stepped into the museum of my own past, and what I found there nearly crushed me" (303). Like Blue, he is not willing to accept Fanshawe's existence. When he is contacted by Fanshawe's wife Sophie to become his literary executor and carry out his will (Oedipa Maas and *The Crying of Lot 49* say hello again!) he is already aware of his dilemma: "Even before I stepped into the apartment, I knew that Fanshawe *had to be* dead [my italics]" (237). The narrator, however, feels frustrated in his attempts to find physical evidence of Fanshawe, who is only present in his books and in the letter he sends to the narrator. Fanshawe's disappearance into another one of his 'boxes'--although this time it seems to be for good, since nobody knows where he is--constitutes the case's cause and its beginning. The narrator's identity is coupled with that of Fanshawe's. Thus, the search for the vanished friend is also a search for the narrator's identity, because like Black and Blue, the narrator and Fanshawe are inseparable. The connection between the two men is also obvious by a strikingly physical similarity. When the narrator visits Fanshawe's mother, she points out that "you even look like him, you know. You always did, the two of you--like brothers, almost like twins. I remember how when you were both small I would sometimes confuse you from a distance. I couldn't tell which one of you was mine" (308). The narrator is again mistaken for Fanshawe during his stay in Paris while meeting one of Fanshawe's old acquaintances. "The resemblance had been noticed before, of course, but never so viscerally, with such immediate impact" (341). In their childhood days, their mutual affection goes so far that they want to get married, since "we were so attached to each other. We wanted to live together when we grew up, and who else but married people did that?" (252). In a way this dream has come true for the narrator as he lives with the ever-present Fanshawe in his mind. The dream, however, seems to have changed into a nightmare. Even when Sophie and the narrator fall in love with each other and establish a relationship, "Fanshawe was still there with us, the unspoken link, the invisible force that had brought us together. It would take some time before he disappeared (...)" (267). The problem is that Fanshawe will not disappear but live on in the narrator's memory and, as he will later find out, in the 'real' world as well, since he is very much alive. Not even his new relationship with Sophie enables the narrator to leave his self-less-ness.

> I began to feel as though I belonged to everyone else as well. My true place in the world (...) was somewhere beyond myself, and if that place was inside me, it was also unlocatable. This was the tiny hole between self and not-self, and for the first time in my life I saw this nowhere as the exact center of the world (274/75).

Again, postmodern 'nothingness' and indeterminacy lurk behind one of Auster's protagonists. Marc Chénetier interpretes this gap, "this intermediary zone--what we might call a 'no-self-land'--[as something that] keeps growing and the white space it defines is the place where everything--destiny, meaning, relation to the Other, language--reaches a vanishing point: this is where the unassignable reigns, the Real."[143] The writing of Fanshawe's biography is an attempt on the narrator's side to re-create his own self by re-constructing the life of the Other. Yet, he has to find out that this project turns out to be a deception.

> We imagine the real story inside the words, and to do this we substitute ourselves for the person in the story, pretending that we can understand him because we understand ourselves. This is a deception. We exist for ourselves, perhaps, and at times we even have a glimmer of who we are, but in the end we can never be sure, and as our lives go on, we become more and more opaque to ourselves, more and more aware of our own incoherence. No one can cross the boundary into another--for the simple reason that no one can gain access to himself (276).

To "substitute" oneself for the person in the "story", hence, the biography, cannot be successful, for one would have to know one's self in order to know the Other and this proves to be impossible. Since, according to Sartre, for one to be, there must be another one,[144] the one is always dependent upon the Other and thus an endless quest for one's own identity must consequently be condemned to fail. Auster creates a postmodern world of incoherence, fragmentation and self-less-ness, which forces his characters to exist like dangling puppets in an endless void, being "no more than an invisible instrument" (263), blindly searching for the Other.

To escape this state of mind, the narrator--like Blue in G--harbors thoughts of killing his double, the only possible way to free himself of Fanshawe's shadow. This

---

[143] Marc Chénetier, "Paul Auster's Pseudonymous World" in: Dennis Barone (ed.), *Beyond the Red Notebook* (Philadelphia: University of Pennsylvania Press, 1995), p. 38.

[144] Jean-Paul Sartre, *Existentialism*, Trans. Bernard Frechtman (New York: Philosophical Library, 1947). "In order to get any truth about myself, I must have contact with another person. The Other is indispensable to my own existence, as well as to my knowledge about myself. This being so, in discovering my inner being I discover the other person at the same time, like a freedom placed in front of us which thinks and wills only for or against me" (44-45).

happens for the first time as he ponders about publishing the work of his missing friend. "I had been given the power to obliterate, to steal a body from its grave and tear it to pieces" (262). His oedipal, sexual encounter with Fanshawe's mother, again triggers the wish within him to kill Fanshawe. "I wanted to kill Fanshawe. I wanted Fanshawe to be dead, and I was going to do it. I was going to track him down and kill him" (315). He needs to find him, to speak to him, to confront him, in order to rid himself not only of the mental but also of the physical presence Fanshawe 'represents'.

The double relationship between the two is marked by yet another reversal of murderous thoughts and death. Now, the narrator, from a distant position ("in the end" [317]), reports that "the strange thing was not that I might have wanted to kill Fanshawe, but that I sometimes imagined he *wanted* me to kill him" (317). This can be explained by Fanshawe's letter, in which he threatens the narrator to kill him "if by some miracle you manage to track me down" (281). He so provokes the narrator to begin the search for him. The constant change between a complete self and the detached and complicated relation to others as well as to his writing (which will be discussed in detail in the next chapter) trap him in the state of a restless wanderer, running away from his own self. Fanshawe never expected his books to be published, because he judged his own work as "garbage" (364), as something that "trapped [him] into what [he] had done (...) and [he] had to wrestle with it all over again" (364). He constantly moves from one 'locked room' to another. From his childhood box, to writing books, to the final setting of his suicide, a house in Boston that he does not leave for more than two years. Yet, with the publication of the books, Fanshawe is forced to leave his 'locked room', to inform the narrator about his existence so that he might finally reveal his struggle to somebody who understands, somebody he can trust.

The narrator, as Fanshawe's double, has the same feelings: "I signed the contract, and afterwards I felt like a man who had signed away his soul" (291). Fanshawe "had chosen me as his executioner, and he knew that he could trust me to carry out the job" (318). To his own horror, he must find out that "the locked room (...) was located inside my skull" (344/45), a fact that irreversibly links him with Fanshawe. The matter becomes even more complicated when the narrator realises his own failure. "Fanshawe was there, and no matter how hard I tried not to think about him, I couldn't escape. (...) I felt as if I was the one who-had been found. Instead of looking for Fanshawe, I had actually been running away from him" (344). Fanshawe deliberately ends his existence through suicide, not being able to overcome the turmoil within himself, which has been created by his knowing about the publication of his books. This reminds him of his role as an author, something that "belongs to another life" (281). He can only find distance from himself through death, since death means solitude. And "solitude became a passageway into the self, an instrument of discovery" (327). Fanshawe experiences this "while living in France [where] he did not hide (...) that he was a writer" (326), a time in which Fanshawe lived the life of a hermite, a life of complete inwardness. Hence, his wish to end his life and enter the solitude of the self that enables him to be a writer once more.

Fanshawe's power over his former friend almost forces the narrator into his own death, when he relives Fanshawe's life during his investigations in America and Paris, including the fight with Stillman, alias Fanshawe. "I learned to live with him in the same way I lived with the thought of my own death. Fanshawe himself was not death--but he was like death, and he functioned as a trope for death inside me" (355). Yet, he finally seems to come to terms with his own identity when he finds out that he has to survive in order to live and let Fanshawe go.

> Fanshawe's power had to be broken, not submitted to. The point was to prove to him that I no longer cared (...). But before I proved this to Fanshawe, I had to prove it to myself, and the fact that I needed to prove it was proof that I still cared too much. It was not enough for me to let things take their course. I had to shake them up, bring them to a head. Because I still doubted myself, I needed to run risks, to test myself before the greatest possible danger. Killing Fanshawe would mean nothing. The point was to find him alive--and then walk away from him alive (317/18).

In the end, however, Auster leaves us with no proofs at all. On the surface, Fanshawe and the nameless narrator for once seem to succeed in what they have been aiming for: Fanshawe commits suicide to enter his own and death's solitude; and the nameless narrator leaves Boston physically alive. However, ultimately, both seem to have failed in their efforts. The red notebook, left behind by Fanshawe to clarify his motivations, is not of any help for the narrator to re-establish his self. The notebook rather conveys another suicide on Fanshawe's side: the self-destruction of the words that "cancel each other out" (370).

> I lost my way after the first word, and from then on I could only grope ahead, faltering in the darkness, blinded by the book that had been written for me. And yet, underneath this confusion, I felt there was something too willed, something too perfect, as though in the end the only thing he had really wanted was to fail--even to the point of failing himself (370).

The nameless narrator has *not* left Fanshawe behind the "double(!)" (359) doors, where he has been hiding from the world. Anne Holzapfel correctly summarises that Fanshawe will remain present in the narrator's self through Sophie and Ben.[145] The narrator's letter box is synonymous with Fanshawe's box, in the same way as the narrator's future and identity may be of a similar 'Fanshawe-nature'. "This was my hiding place, the one spot in the world that was purely my own. And yet it linked me to the rest of the world, and in its magic darkness there was the power to make things happen" (280). Possibly, it holds true what we are told by the nameless narrator about one's identity: "You get to a certain point in life, and then it's too late to change" (324). Or in other words, "once it happens, it goes on happening; you live with it for the rest of your life" (356). Paul Auster, judging his own text, feels tempted to provide us with a more positive outlook on the narrator's identity. "But in the end, he manages to resolve the question for himself--more or less. He finally comes to accept his own life, to understand that no matter how bewitched or haunted he is, he has to accept reality as it is, to tolerate the presence of ambiguities within himself."[146]

Nathaniel Hawthorne, a source of which Auster preferably makes use, as discussed in the chapter on intertextuality, may serve as our own source for judging the aspect of identity in Auster's detective fiction. "By stepping aside for a moment, a man exposes himself to a fearful risk of losing his place forever."[147] Quinn, Blue, and the nameless narrator are all Wakefields who have stepped away from their daily life, trying to take over their doubles' identities--Stillman's, Black's and Fanshawe's, all Wakefields as well--only to lose their new identities along the way and disappear in the postmodern void of incoherence, nothingness and fragmentation.

---

[145] cf. Holzapfel, p. 94.

[146] Paul Auster, *The Art of Hunger*, p. 264.

[147] Nathaniel Hawthorne, "Wakefield", in: *The Celestial Railroad and Other Stories* (New York: Penguin, 1980), p. 75.

Each text is a machine with multiple
reading heads for other texts.
--Jacques Derrida--

5 Concepts of Reading and Writing: The Death of (the) Author(ity)? or Detecting the Postmodern Text

The headline of this chapter seems to convey a postulation of postmodern aesthetics in itself: plurality. But how, the reader may ask, are we to understand such different and complex aspects of postmodern literature within a single chapter, and how are we to examine all of these aspects in Auster's trilogy? There seems to be a rather simple answer to this question. Detective fiction, despite its reality claims, is also a matter of convention and therefore a product of textuality, a text. We assume then that the trilogy is a postmodern text, which is of course part of the overall thesis that places the trilogy within the genre of postmodern detective fiction. Second, a literary text, quite generally, has to do with reading and writing. Third, a piece of text needs an author, and an author makes use of characters, narrative concepts (i.e. point of view) and thus imposes his own authority on the text. With Auster, it is a different case. To stress the complexity of the human subject, its constantly shifting nature, and the indeterminacy prevalent in today's world, Auster often makes unclear the ontologically distinct categories of author, artist, narrator, and character. The connections between author, narrator, character (and the character's relation with other characters, as well as their relation to the reader) are not as simple as in a traditional detective novel, in which binary associations are prevalent. Out of this, several questions arise: Who narrates the trilogy? What is Paul Auster's role within his own novels? How can we account for the several overlapping layers of text, inherent within the NYT? What is the role of the reader, and who is the reader? Who is the author of the text and who or what imposes authority on the characters? What consequences does writing have for the characters and for the world as such? One could, I suppose, find many more questions aiming in this direction. The questions mentioned above are closely related to questions we might raise on the level of detective fiction. Who is the actual reader of clues? Who is the observing and who is being observed? Is there a relation between writing, reading and detecting, and between writer and detective? How many authors, readers and writers do we meet in the NYT? The names and interrelations of the narrators of the three novels are complex and paradoxical. Some characters are twinned, some are revealed to be imaginary figures invented by other characters, some appear in one book, only to appear in the next book with a different identity, and so forth. How is the reader to maintain any coherence of this complexity, if not outright contradiction? By concentrating on the aspects and questions mentioned above, this paper shows how Auster employs and subverts such fundamental concepts of literature, as reading and writing, character, author(ity), narratology, structure and plot. Story-telling is not destroyed but certainly deconstructed. For this chapter, a separate examination of each story is not intended because cross-references between the three novels during the discussion of each concept serve to clarify aspects that hold true for each story.

5.1 The Question of Author(ity)

Auster leaves the reader wondering where fiction begins and non-fiction ends. Quite often there is no clear distinction between a narrator that is telling the story and the author who is writing it, between fictional characters created exclusively for the work and celebrities, writers and other 'real' people, between imagined events and actual occurrences. The reader cannot really accept any one character with the knowledge that it is just a construct because it may be a reflection of the artist himself.

In CoG, there is a character named Paul Auster, who is also a writer. Is this character now not a character at all but the writer of the novel we are reading? The crux is that there is not one true answer to such questions because that would contradict what postmodernism is all about. We also have another character, Quinn, who is a writer but strives to have an extratextual adventure that would supplement and enhance his fascination with writing about detectives. However, writing and detecting soon become one and the same thing, since "seeing the thing and writing about it [is] the same fluid gesture" (77). Quinn returns to writing, understanding that "in the end, it was the red notebook that offered him salvation" (75).

Through the complex, multi-faceted works we are reminded that reality itself is often complex, multi-faceted, and subject to interpretation. The indeterminacy and ever-fluctuating nature of life is stressed by Auster through creating indeterminacy in his work. This, combined with a conviction that the author is no longer the supreme authority or interpreter of the human, cultural and social condition, accounts for the lack of omniscience, tightly controlled plots, well-developed characters, and linear storylines. Literature's autonomy and writings' "essential drift is (...) cut off from all absolute responsibility or from consciousness as the ultimate authority, orphaned and separated at birth from the assistance of its father."[148] In CoG, the novel's opening faulty connection "is a desperate critical effort, made by an other reader at the very moment the book is cracked (open), to establish a primal unity for the work by locating an original literary site, to reach the Author at a permanent address. But in this errant text, the author is never at home."[149] In the same way as the traditional detective novel presumes a structure and a case in which nothing goes to waste since everything turns out to conform to a central, organising logos or author-itative cause, its postmodern deviation negates such an ultimate author-ity behind everything. The "global village" of our time cannot be reflected in well-structured, linear movements, but rather in a multilayered text, in which the boundaries between fiction and reality, character, narrator and author, victim and culprit seem to be in a constant 'postmodern' flow. Alison Russell points out that in Auster's work "each text denies any *one* meaning or solution" [my italics],[150] smoothing the way for endless possibilities and deviations of literary norms.

In CoG, we are told why detectives and writers play such a crucial role in the trilogy. "The detective is one who looks, who listens, who moves through this morass of objects and events in search of the thought, the idea that will pull all these things together and make sense of them. In effect, the writer and the detective are interchangeable" (9). We know that Quinn is a writer and not a detective, we also know that Auster is a writer and no detective, yet through the detective they are connected. Auster, however, by being "both outside and inside the novel,"[151] imposes

---

[148] Jacques Derrida, "Signature, Event, Context", in: *Limited Inc.* (Evanston: Northwestern University Press, 1988), p. 8.
[149] Little, p. 153.
[150] Russell, p. 72.
[151] Russell, p. 73.

and takes away authority and knowledge at the same time, thus creating the postmodern void, in which Quinn blindly staggers for meaning and a solution. The character Paul Auster replies to Quinn, who is looking for the private detective Auster he himself impersonates, that "I'm afraid you've got the wrong Paul Auster", leaving Quinn in total puzzlement, as "you're the only one in the book" (113). Let us not forget the one outside the book. But is this the 'real' Auster? An answer to that question, or to the meaning of the text in general, however, is not granted. Neither to Quinn, nor to the reader, since the "center is everywhere, and no circumference can be drawn until the book has come to its end" (9). Through this, the reader is forced to participate in the process of detection if he is out for a possible solution. We follow the narrator's account, presented to us from Quinn's point of view, stick close to the case, stagger along with Quinn, Blue, and the rest of the aimless wanderers only to be told by the nameless narrator in TLR that

> the entire story comes down to what happened at the end, and without that end inside me now, I could not have started this book. The same holds true for the two books that come before it, *City of Glass* and *Ghosts*. These three stories are finally the same story, but each one represents a different stage in my awareness of what it is about. I don't claim to have solved any problems. I am merely suggesting that a moment came when it no longer frightened me to look at what had happened. If words followed, it was only because I had no choice but to accept them, to take them upon myself and go where they wanted me to go. But that does not necessarily make the words important. I have been struggling to say good-bye to something for a long time now, and this struggle is all that really matters. The story is not in the words; it's in the struggle (346).

Here, the narrator claims authorship for all three of the novels, surprising the reader with his announcement that, basically, we have read the same story three times, told from different points of view with different characters but essentially, only with a different "awareness of what it is about." The arbitrariness of the words "that followed" from this awareness is the reason why there are three different stories, implying that the same words never produce the same story. Alternatively, a limited set of words creates an unlimited number of stories, strengthening the notion that the trilogy is also a book about the impossibility of a closed text. The words themselves are unimportant, since "the question is the story itself, and whether or not it means something is not for the story to tell" (3). "Trying to impose meaning on the text, to interpret it, has become the unforgivable crime, the story does not permit any investigation/interpretation, and the reader who is trying to do so is finally the criminal."[152] Or, as Sweeney puts it, "every narrative exploits a constant tension between meaning (the anticipated revelation of a coherent narrative pattern) and meaninglessness (the fear that no such pattern exists)."[153] Freywald is correct in stating that a single coherent meaning cannot be deduced from the text. She is, however, incorrect in claiming that the text does not permit "any investigation/interpretation," since an examination on the textual level of writing can in fact yield useful results.

With the lack of authority comes the lack of responsibility for one's own writing. The story is the most important result of writing, it is there to be there and if no solution is presented then this might be the fault of the characters, the detectives, but not of the author(ity), since there is none present. Quinn turns himself into a detective and becomes the protagonist for Paul Auster, who then becomes a character within the story. Who can we rely on? The narrator claims that he has "been struggling for a long time to say good-bye to something" (346). Does this "good-bye" really describe his farewell to writing? Is this why we have been struggling through his text? And if the story "is not in the words" yet in the struggle, how are we to leave this struggle and find meaning? The answer is that there is no answer. "I don't claim to have solved any problems," any riddles, any cases. There is no end, as there is to reading: rather, there is the hesitating, interminable response of writing. Characters must die in order to live, and stories must be written in order to live on and be written again. The fictitious Auster asks Quinn in CoG: "Are you in the book?" (122), and Quinn replies: "Yes, (...) the only one" (123). For once, Quinn has presented us with a solution. There is only one story out of which Auster creates more, although he might 'suffer' from what Roland Barthes termed 'The Death of the Author': "To give a text an author is to impose a limit on that text, to furnish it with a final signified, to close the writing."[154] Paul Auster leaves the writing open. This strategy seems to mirror Jean-Francois Lyotard's view of the postmodern writer and artist: "[They] are working without rules in order to formulate the rules of what *will*

---

[152] Freywald, p. 157.

[153] S. E. Sweeney, "Locked Rooms: Detective Fiction, Narrative Theory and Self-Reflexivity", in: Ronald Walker et al. (eds.), *The Cunning Craft: Original Essays on Detective Fiction and Contemporary Literary Theory* (Macomb: Western Illinois University Press, 1990), p. 4.

[154] Roland Barthes, "The Death of the Author", *Image--Music--Text* (London: Fontana, 1977), p.147.

have been done [emphasis Lyotard's]."[155] The art will be discovered in "what will have been done," in making something from anything rather than reacting against what is traditional, conventional or normative. It is anything that can be made into a text, which is even more than 'anything goes'. Furthermore, Auster creates a new text, a text that seems to exist without a clear author(ity), reflecting what Michel Foucault has observed as the fact that "we are at present witnessing the disappearance of the figure of the 'great writer'."[156]

5.2 Concepts of Writing

The trilogy keeps "recycling references to itself,"[157] cross-references between volumes, concerning characters, the red notebook, and historical and fictitious figures. Yet, writing as such is an ever-present concern in the trilogy. Protagonists are busy with the writing of some report, of a fictional biography, of appearing and disappearing notebooks. Writing is possible without being able to speak and hear, as we are reminded when Quinn buys a pen from a deaf-mute (63). He buys a pen and a notebook to write in, since "it would be helpful to have a separate place to record his thoughts, his observations, and his questions. In that way, perhaps, things might not get out of control" (46). The first thing we learn about Auster is that he is a man with "an uncapped fountain pen, still poised in a writing position" (111), and Black opens the door for Blue, "standing in the doorway with an uncapped fountain pen in his right hand, as though interrupted in his work" (218). Writing is self-reflexively interwoven into the text, a sort of 'meta-writing' in a meta-fictional detective story: writing as an attempt to acquire knowledge, to find one's own self, as Black puts it when he explains to Blue what he thinks Blue seems to be doing. "I think he's writing about himself. The story of his life. That's the only possible answer. Nothing else would fit" (215). Although from the perspective of an author, "writing is a solitary

---

[155] Jean-Francois Lyotard, "Answering the Question: What is Postmodernism?", in: Ihab and Sally Hassan (eds.), *Innovation/Renovation: New Perspectives on the Humanities* (Madison: University of Wisconsin Press, 1983), pp. 340/41.

[156] Michel Foucault, "Truth and Power", in: *Power/Knowledge*, trans. Colin Gordon (New York: Pantheon Books, 1980), p. 27.

[157] Marc Chénetier, p. 39.

business", which "takes over your life" (209), writing can also be the equivalent of life, "a big book", something Black has "been working on (...) for many years" and to Blue 's question, whether he was almost finished, he replies: "I'm getting there (...). But sometimes it's hard to know where you are. I think I'm almost done, and then I realise I've left out something important, and so I have to go back to the beginning again. But yes, I do dream of finishing it one day" (220). Black will only be finished with his book when he has died. "In some sense a writer has no life of his own. Even when he's there, he's not really there" (209). In how far these experiences can be traced back to the 'real' life of the writer Paul Auster is probably not the question here. What we learn from the impersonal narrator about Quinn and his 'essence of writing' comes close to what Auster might have aimed at with these detective novels. "What interested him about the stories he wrote was not their relation to the world but their relation to other stories" (8). Writing is something so terribly important and gripping that it is possible to take over one's life. The results, however, can be found in many of Auster's characters: frustration, the inability to distinguish between the real world and fiction, and identity problems.

5.3 Writing and Author(ity) in *City of Glass*

Writing is by nature closely connected to the aspect of author(ity) and authorship. By taking a closer look at CoG, which deconstructs the traditional form of the novel most obviously--and later deconstructs itself by literally falling apart in its progression--and by concentrating on the *mise-en-abyme*--the self-reflexive repetition of the novel's structure in the scene in which Auster and Quinn meet and talk about Don Quixote--the question of authorship, point of view and postmodern subversion of the novel shall be examined examined in more detail. Cross-references to G and TLR will be included in the discussion.

Let us first turn to a consideration of the novel's point of view. A figural third-person point of view with loosely scattered explanations to the reader is maintained almost all the way to the end of the novel when an "enigmatic 'I' suddenly reveals itself."[158] A friend of the fictitious Auster comes back from a trip to Africa and is notified by Auster about the case, Quinn and the notebook, which they find in Stillman's apartment:

> I have followed the red notebook as closely as I could, and any inaccuracies in the story should be blamed on me. There were moments when the text was difficult to decipher, but I have done my best with it and have refrained from any interpretation. The red notebook, of course, is only half the story, as any sensitive reader will understand (158).

Frankly, the reader probably does not understand this at all. We are confronted with a highly unreliable narrator, who is telling us only half the story (where is the other half?), and who admits in the middle of the novel that "the account of this period is less full than the author would have liked. But information is scarce, and he has preferred to pass over in silence what could not be definitely confirmed" (135). The narrator even goes as far as claiming that "this story is based entirely on facts" and thus he "feels it his duty not to overstep the bounds of the verifiable, to resist at all costs the perils of invention" (135). Having said this, he admits that "even the red notebook, which until now has provided a detailed account of Quinn's experiences, is suspect. We cannot say for certain what happened to Quinn (...), for it is at this point of the story that he began to lose his grip" (135). Outright contradictions and helpless concessions to the reader make the narrator's account of Quinn's case a doubtful one.

Early in the novel, the narrator plays with the reader's perception of truth, when the introduction of Marco Polo's *Travels* is quoted. "We will set down things seen as seen, things heard as heard, so that our book may be an accurate record, free from any sort of fabrication. And all who read this book or hear it may do so with full confidence, because it contains nothing but the truth" (7). The reader, like Quinn, is "beginning to ponder the meaning of these sentences, to turn their crisp assurances over in his mind" (7). Trying to find out the truth, Quinn enters his own fiction and slowly loses the feeling for reality. Even the red notebook, that is supposed to serve him as a guarantor of order, ensuring that "things might not get out of order" (46), cannot be the absolute source of truth. While following Stillman Sr, Quinn learns to position both notebook and pen in such a way that he can observe Stillman carefully and record his observations at the same time. He is, however, only "producing a

---

[158] William Lavender, "The Novel of Critical Engagement: Paul Auster's *City of Glass*", *Contemporary Literature* 34:2, 1993, p. 220.

81

jumbled, illegible palimpsest" (76), on which the narrator then has to construct his story. Clearly, Quinn uses the notebook in order to get the "real story", to transcribe reality, to find out the truth and to master it at the same time. There is, however, no reality and no truth, but only text. Or, if there is reality, then it has already been turned into a text, since the notebook contains the only record of the case. In the end, there is only the notebook. As Malmgren points out correctly: "Quinn tried to pretend to be a Work, but he was condemned to be a Text."[159] Story-telling and narrative structure are deconstructed from 'within': the blending of different narrative situations (a figural one from Quinn's point of view, a first-person narrator who claims to have reconstructed Quinn's story by means of the red notebook, and traces of authorial intrusions in form of explanations to the reader [cf. p. 135 in CoG]) does not allow for neat and tidy distinctions and rather creates fragmentation, de-centralisation and the impossibility of a solution as elements can no longer be put together or related to each other.

> *City of Glass* suggests, allegorically, a hopelessly complex, paradoxical, self-referential system of geneses that parodies (...) the very idea of models of narrative structure by making itself into a model of itself. We could say that it naively takes the critics at their word, writes itself according to the plan, the critical blueprint, even takes it a step further (if three layers are good, shouldn't six, or ten, be better?), and erects the lopsided monument of its structure as the most eloquent comment on the theory.[160]

Auster further complicates the situation by his making use of the *mise-en-abyme* technique. When Quinn meets Auster, they talk about *Don Quixote* about whom Auster is writing an essay, which "has to do with the authorship of the book. Who wrote it, and how it was written" (116). It is the "book inside the book Cervantes wrote, the one he imagined he was writing" (117), and it is the book inside the book which we, the actual readers, are being confronted with. Auster's speculations about the authorship of Don Quixote clearly have reverberations for the model of authorship enacted in CoG. CoG is a reworking of *Don Quixote*, a book that also denies its own authority while claiming to be a true story. In showing that Sancho Panza is the real author of the book, Auster is self-reflexively accounting for his own 'abuse' of traditional narrative theory. His theory, in effect, writes Cervantes entirely

---

[159] Carl D. Malmgren, "Detecting/Writing the Real: Paul Auster's *City of Glass*", in: Theo D'haen and Hans Bertens (eds.), *Narrative Turns and Minor Genres in Postmodernism* (Amsterdam: Rodopi, 1995), p. 197.
[160] Lavender, p. 224.

out of the picture. Madeleine Sorapure writes that "Don Quixote serves as a kind of 'center elsewhere' in the world of the work: completely visible throughout the work as its enigmatic main character, yet nowhere visible as its mastermind and master plotter."[161] Auster is visible as a character in the work but not as its "mastermind," to echo Sorapure's words. It is interesting to note that Quinn (Auster) is referred to the Stillmanns through "Mrs. Saavedra's (Peter's nurse) husband, Michael (35). So, in a way, Miguel de Cervantes Saavedra has a 'cameo-role' in CoG.

Cervantes (the real one now!) claims in his book that the text was originally written in Arabic by Cid Hamete Benengeli. Cervantes then happened to find it on the Toledo market, had it translated, and then presented himself as the editor of the translation.[162] According to Auster in CoG, Cervantes argues that this version "is the only true version" and thus "had to claim that it was real" (117). Auster then goes on to say that in order to prove the truthful account of the story, it "has to be written by an eyewitness to the events" (117). Cid Hamete Benengeli, however, "never makes an appearance" (118) and is thus a pastiche of four people: the illiterate Sancho Panza, who is also the only witness to Quixote's adventures, the barber and the priest, to whom Sancho has told the story and who put the story "into a proper literary form- -in Spanish" (118), and Samson Carrasco who then translated it into Arabic. Later, Cervantes discovered the book, and arranged to have it translated and published. So far so good. However, Auster still has another ace up his sleeve. By inventing this ploy, Sancho and his friend only wanted to "cure Don Quixote ["a stand-in for Cervantes" (117)] of his madness" (118). Quixote, however, according to Auster in the novel, "was not really mad, he only pretended to be. In fact, he orchestrated the whole thing himself" (119). That implies knowledge on his side, namely that his chronicler, Sancho Panza exists, "whom Don Quixote has chosen for exactly this purpose" (119): to record his own story.

> It was Don Quixote who engineered the Benengeli quartet. And not only did he select
> the authors, it was probably he who translated the Arabic manuscript back into Spanish.

---

[161] Madeleine Sorapure, "The Detective and the Author" in: Dennis Barone (ed.), *Beyond the Red Notebook* (Philadelphia: University of Pennsylvania Press, 1995), p. 84.

[162] The *Name of the Rose* by Umberto Eco, another postmodern detective story, works in a similar way. In *Constructing Postmodernism*, Brian McHale tells us that the world of *The Name of the Rose* and thus the text has been mediated by four intermediaries: "first Adso, whose text has been edited by Mabillon, whose text in turn has been translated by Vallet, whose text has in its turn been 'transcribed' by Eco." [Brian McHale, "The (Post)modernism of *The Name of the Rose*", in: *Constructing Postmodernism* (New York: Routledge, 1992), p. 155.]

> (...) I like to imagine that scene in the marketplace at Toledo. Cervantes hiring Don Quixote to decipher the story of Don Quixote himself. There's great beauty to it (119).

If one has attentively followed Auster's elaboration on *Don Quixote* and the question of authorship, there is only one solution to this question. Sancho Panza, a character in a novel, is at the same time its author.

Steven Alford constructs a different and very interesting pattern for the 'Quixote-case' in his essay "Mirrors of Madness: Paul Auster's *New York Trilogy*".[163] He examines the account of Quixote under a different light, suggesting "{Auster}" to be the narrator and claims that the story has been invented for {Auster} by some concerned friends, such as a 'real' Quinn (as Sancho Panza), and the Stillmans (parallels to the other three friends). According to Alford, his friends intended to cure {Auster} from his madness and invented the whole ploy. To follow {Auster's} argument in the story, it could well be that he had orchestrated the whole thing and chose Quinn as his chronicler, so that he could "spew out lies and nonsense" (119) for people's amusement. Hence, we have Paul Auster, the author of CoG, as well as the writer in CoG, who is himself a character invented by {Paul Auster}, narrator, the same way that the character 'Don Quixote' was engineered by Don Quixote. Alford then writes: "Of course, Don Quixote never existed, but was invented by Miguel de Cervantes Saavedra of Spain. By association, {Paul Auster} never existed, but was an invention of the 'real' Paul Auster, of Manhattan."[164] That leaves us with three Austers: author, narrator, and character, each ontologically different.

Madeleine Sorapure[165] yet suggests another theory, in which she claims that Auster (the character), in order to test his theory himself, invented Quinn, wrote the red notebook himself, passed it on to the narrator with some fictitious background, in order to have him write the novel. Sorapure places Auster, as author, in an even greater position of mastery and authority, something she calls "a kind of metamastery"[166], a place behind the events and the characters in the novel and behind the writing of the novel itself.

---

[163] Steven Alford, "Mirrors of Madness: Paul Auster's *New York Trilogy*", Critique 37:1, 1995, pp. 17-33.
[164] Alford, p. 21.
[165] Sorapure, "The Detective and the Author", pp. 71-85.
[166] Sorapure, p. 85.

Postmodern plurality reigns in the realm of narrative situation. In his postmodern text, Auster (the real author!) is intensively subverting our general perception of narrative discourse. By blurring the functions of character, narrator and author, he only offers postmodern fragmentation, which is a 'doubtful certainty' for the reader'. The story itself is not a closed system that claims a definite truth about who really is the author(ity) within the text. As we know, Quinn adopts still more pseudonyms in the course of the story, e.g. Daniel Quinn, Stillman Jr, and Henry Dark, which complicates the issue even more. "And around and around it goes" (122), Daniel Auster correctly comments on that absurd situation. Alison Russell describes Quinn as a "paper Auster, a mere linguistic construct of the author himself."[167] Quinn is not aware that he is Auster's creation, telling Stillman Jr. on the phone, that "there is no Paul Auster here" (8). Quinn wonders about the time, his initial interview with Stillman Jr. has taken. "Apparently, a whole day had gone by" (27), although his appointment was for 10 a.m. And a little later, he finds out that "he had been there for more than fourteen hours. Within himself, however, it felt as though his stay had lasted three or four hours at most" (43). He cannot know that taking over the case means entering text time, in which experimental time equals writing time. The interview takes as long as it takes the chapter to be written, namely fourteen hours. Furthermore, Russell reads in Quinn's eagerness to slip into Auster's skin, a "pursuit of the father, [the] search for authority and 'author-ity'."[168] Quinn desperately tries to be a 'Father' for Stillman Jr., a fatherless (authorless) young man, a "marionette trying to walk without strings" (17). He is a "puppet boy" trying to "grow up and become real" (26). Stillman was hoping for Auster (an author), not knowing who he is or how to exist, but he only gets Quinn (a character). "Perhaps, I am Peter Stillman, and perhaps I am not" (23). Lavender writes that "Peter has sent for Auster his author to save his life. Without his author, he must remain in darkness, unknown, off the page, his name cannot be 'real'. But Quinn is only a character; he cannot save him. Peter Stillman walks off page 28 and never returns."[169] Quinn is also unable to solve the mystery and is thus doubly stripped of his authority: Of the detective's authority, and of the one as a character, who has to find out that the author

---

[167] Russell, p. 73.
[168] Russell, p. 74.
[169] Lavender, pp. 226/27.

(Auster) is only a character, which himself is impersonated by Quinn. All of the author-characters in the novel--Quinn, Stillman, Auster, and the narrator--"try to apply the logic of the traditional detective story to their experiences as detectives, and instead realise, in varying degrees, the inadequacy and inaccuracy of the genre's presuppositions."[170] What they seem to be gaining through their writing and their detective work is only fragmented and imperfect understanding. For Quinn, the name Auster is a mere husk without content. "As Auster he could not summon up any memories or fears, any dreams or joys, for all these things, as they pertained to Auster, were a blank to him. He consequently had to remain solely on his own surface, looking outward for sustenance" (75). What remains for Quinn on his search for author(ity), and for the reader on the search for a solution, is to define fate as the condition of things and events as they are and take place.

> Fate in the sense of what was, of what happened to be. It was something like the word 'it' in the phrase 'it is raining' or 'it is night.' What that 'it' referred to Quinn has never known. A generalised condition of things as they were, perhaps; the state of is-ness that was the ground on which the happenings of the world took place. He could not be any more definite than that. But perhaps he was not really searching for anything definite (133).

In the end, Quinn no longer feels to be part of his triad of selves, which means that he has lost the last solid ground for him to stand on. "He remembered the books he had written under the name of William Wilson. It was strange, he thought, that he had done that, and he wondered now why he had. In his heart, he realized that Max Work was dead" (153). He has lost the perspective on his case, he is beyond, above it, and thus beyond his quest for author(ity). CoG calls into question the function of the author as fundamental ground and reassuring certitude in the world of the fiction. The equation author=authority in postmodern detective fiction does not hold true. For some closing insights on the question of authorship, the paper briefly considers the other two stories of the trilogy.

---

[170] Sorapure, p. 73.

5.4 Writing and Author(ity) in *Ghosts*

Ghosts begins on February 3, 1947, continuing through midsummer of 1948. However, it also begins with a contradiction when we are told by the narrator that "the time is the present" (161) only to be reminded that it is actually the year 1947. If we enter the fictional level of the book and try to correctly solve the question of authorship and narrator, we again run into some problems, since G is in the narrative present. Let us proceed with some detective work. Through the evidence in CoG, which was written between 1981 and 1982, and with Quinn 35 years old, and Auster (the character) around the same age, Auster would have been born around the beginning of the narrative time of G. By some very peculiar coincidence, Auster's birthday is on February 3, 1947; but how can you write a detective story as an infant? The first-person narrator in TLR claims authorship for all three stories, and this paper states in chapter 4 that we are to take Paul Auster as the narrator of all three stories. This is obviously against the basic rule of narratology, which is never to consider author and narrator as the same person. Since the narrative world of the NYT seems to be beyond all perception and laws of narratology (or at least subverts a coherent understanding of narratology), as we have seen above, we may as well stick to this assumption for the moment, as long as we understand both the terms 'narrator' and 'author' as standing for what Alford calls "a locus of textual space, one which nominally includes you, me, and Paul Auster, author."[171] That would make Auster a new-born infant in G and 35 years old in CoG. From the textual evidence, both assumptions seem to be correct. Of course, this is against any empirical laws and against our perception of what is possible. If we, however, have another close look at the passage in TLR, in which the narrator writes that "each one [of the 3 stories] represents a different state in my awareness of what it is about" (346), then we could assume that Auster places his awareness of the story into the days of his childhood, echoing the narrator's mental excursions into his own past in TLR. This argument is strengthened by Steven Alford who writes that "it seems reasonable to assume that the narrator of Ghosts is {Auster} [the character Auster], who is establishing for

---

[171] Alford, "Mirrors of Madness", p. 27.

himself an imaginative narrative space around the time of his birth."[172] Like in CoG, *Ghosts* suddenly brings about a shift in the narrative discourse. It begins in third person omniscient and ends with the intrusion of a first person narrator. Yet, it differs from CoG in this respect that the narrator does not have the position of another character, but rather includes the reader in his comment.

> Where he [Blue] goes after that is not important. For *we* [my italics] must remember that all his took place more than thirty years ago, back in the days of our earliest childhood. Anything is possible, therefore. I myself prefer to think that he went far away, boarding a train that morning and going out West to start a new life (232).

By using the first person plural, Auster invites us to remember our own childhood, seeing the story from a different perspective, a new awareness. Auster, the narrator, is the fictional 'ghost' of the author Auster, which is also reflected in the 'ghost-like' structure of the novel: colors instead of names, indeterminacy and indifference towards places and events, and the presence of 'literary ghosts' such as Hawthorne and Whitman. Russell states that "the 'meat' of the text is stripped down to a generic level, reinforced by Auster's rejection of nomenclature and his use of Film Noir signifiers."[173] The writer, and thus the author, is a ghost, leading a "solitary life", being "not really there (...), when he's there" (209). This adequatly expresses the question of author(ity) in *Ghosts*. Being there, but at the same time not being there.

Alsen, however, has a different view concerning the author(ity) of *Ghosts*. He suggests that what we have been reading is a story written by Black, and that only the two last paragraphs are written by a different narrator. Alsen argues that Blue is the narrator, who writes the concluding parts of the story to throw the authorities off his track. His thesis is based on three passages in the text. When Blue returns with the manuscript he has stolen from Black's apartment, "he reads the story right through, every word from beginning to end" (232). As he is reading the manuscript, we are told by the narrator that "time is short. They will be coming before he knows it and there will be hell to pay" (232). Thus, Black hopes that Blue will be punished for his murder. In another scene at the beginning of the novel, the narrator says about Blue: "Little does Blue know, of course, that the case will go on for years" (162). But Blue confounds Black's expectations by finishing the case in little more than a year.

---

[172] Alford, p. 26.
[173] Russell, p. 77.

Furthermore, Alsen quotes the passage, in which the narrator talks about the street on which Black lives and mentions that "Walt Whitman handset the first edition of *Leaves of Grass* on this street in 1855" (163). Later, Black passes the same fact along to Blue, saying that "Whitman printed his first book right here, not far from where you're standing" (205).[174] This different approach to the story and its author(ity) seems to confirm my hypothesis that Auster's texts allow for multiple possibilities of author(itie)s and narrators. Perhaps, each of these possibilities "represent a different state in [our] awareness of what [the story] is about" (346). And a different awareness might as well include a different point of view and the uncertainty of the story's author(ity).

5.5 Writing and Author(ity) in *The Locked Room*

TLR is narrated in the first person and opens in May 1984, text time and 'real' time. By indicating the date at the end of his novels, Auster succesfully combines text time and 'real' time, that is here the period of time, in which the story is written. Being the most coherent story among the three in the trilogy, concerning plot, and linear structure, it has not much in stock for our discussion on author(ity) and narrative discourse, besides the revelation on the narrator's side that he claims authorship for the whole trilogy, an aspect, which has been dealt with above. One small passage, however, is relevant. This passage echoes Quinn's thoughts in CoG and is concerned with

> what it means when a writer puts his name on a book, why some writers choose to hide behind a pseudonym, whether or not a writer has a real life anyway. It struck me that writing under another name might be something I would enjoy--to invent a secret identity for myself--and I wondered why I found this idea so attractive (279).

In blurring the boundaries between character, author and narrator so intensively, Auster has actually taken on a "secret identity, a pseudonym" for himself. In true postmodern fashion he experiments with deviations from formerly clear-cut positions

---

[174] Eberhard Alsen, "Paul Auster's *Ghosts* and *Mr. Vertigo*: Homage to the Romantics", *Postmodern Studies 19: Romantic Postmodernism in American Fiction* (Amsterdam: Rodopi, 1996), p. 249.

in a novel, and thus changes our understanding of how narrative discourse in general can be used to convey postmodern aesthetics in a fragmented world.

5.6 The Question of Plot

Let us now briefly turn our attention to the aspect of plot, another part of the narrative art, that, as one could expect in advance, is also subverted by Auster in his trilogy. "The structural components of the ordering imagination--story lines cultivated over centuries of use--are openly interrogated."[175] This section examines the aspect of plot with the help of such standard contributions to this subject as Roland Barthes' "hermeneutic code" in *S/Z*, Tzevtan Todorov's "The Typology of Detective Fiction" in *The Poetics of Prose* and Peter Brook's book *Reading for the Plot*.

The structure of the classic detective novel, depending on sequence, causality, and the possibility of solution in a positivistic universe, fits neatly with one of the five "codes" described by Roland Barthes. The "hermeneutic code" is constituted by "the various (formal) terms by which an enigma can be distinguished, suggested, formulated, held in suspense, and finally disclosed."[176] This process parallels the unravelling and solving of a mystery in a classic detective story. Auster, and the postmodern detective novel in general deny that dependence and work to undermine the hermeneutic code. Dennis Porter points out that the classical detective novel

> is a genre committed to an act of recovery, moving forward in order to move back. The detective encounters effects without apparent causes, events in a jumbled chronological order (...). And his role is to reestablish sequence and causality.[177]

Postmodern detective novels reject the linear and teleological structures of these stories and call causality and linearity into question. As discussed earlier, they also do not offer a satisfying closure. Tzevtan Todorov underlines that the story of detection, which we follow along in the narrative and which is present for the reader, exists to reveal the story of crime, which is unpresent, yet of more importance since it

---

[175] Saltzman, p. 53.

[176] Roland Barthes. *S/Z*, trans. Richard Miller (New York: Hill, 1974), p. 19.

[177] Dennis Porter, *The Pursuit of Crime* (New Haven: Yale University Press, 1981), p. 29f.

bears the actual meaning.[178] He describes the two different stories, inquest and crime, as *sjuzet* (the act of narration) and *fabula* (story), thus making the detective novel "the narrative of narratives, its classical structure a laying-bare of the structure of all narrative in that it dramatises the role of *sjuzet* and *fabula* and the nature of their relation. Plot (...) once more appears as the active process of *szujet* working on *fabula*, the dynamic of its interpretive ordering."[179] In other words, the detective novel is as an allegory for narratives in general. For Brooks, as well as for Peter Hühn, the detective's uncovering of the crime is analogous to the reader's deciphering of the plot.[180] Brooks further argues that the process of detection, in which the "detective repeat[s], go[es] over again the ground that has been covered by his predecessor, the criminal," is inevitably linked to the notion of plot, because "in repeating the steps of the criminal-predecessor, [the detective] is literalizing an act that all narrative claims to perform (...). Narrative ever, and inevitably--if only because of its use of the preterite--presents itself as a repetition and rehearsal (...) of what has already happened."[181] On the surface, Quinn, Blue and the nameless narrator all fulfill their detective duty as they go over the ground the culprits Stillman, Black and Fanshawe have left for them. Their search 'propels the plot' through the narrative. Yet, the deeper they get involved into the case, the plot becomes less clear and coherent.

5.6.1 Plot in *City of Glass*

Quinn begins his surveillance by reading Stillman's dissertation, dealing with, among other things, the 'Tower of Babel' and the aspect of prelapasarian language. He follows Stillman for 13 days, noting down everything in his notebook. As Stillman seems to lack a destination, Quinn must concentrate on the way in which Stillman travels and must hope to find meaning within the navigation process itself. Frustrated

---

[178] cf. Tzevtan Todorov, "The Typology of Detective Fiction", in: *The Poetics of Prose* (Ithaca: Cornell University Press, 1977), pp. 42-52.
[179] Peter Brooks, *Reading for the Plot: Design and Intention in Narrative* (New York: Knopf, 1984), p. 25.
[180] cf. Brooks, pp. 23-29 and Peter Hühn, "The Detective as Reader: Narrativity and Reading Concepts in Detective Fiction", *Modern Fiction Studies* 33:3, 1987, pp. 451-466.
[181] Brooks, p. 25.

by the principle of linear narrative and plot (where is Stillman going?), and by a seeming lack of clues, Quinn sits down with his red notebook and "sketched a little map of the area Stillman had wandered in" (80). The resulting map no longer represents New York, or a neighborhood, and Quinn deduces from his map that the old man's wanderings must be adressed on their own terms as new possibilities arise. William Lavender correctly points out that "'to plot' can also mean 'to map'"[182], and thus Quinn 'plots' Stillman's walks and finds out, although uncertainty never disappears, that the old man is 'walking a word', the TOWER OF BABEL. The problem is, however, that "it could well have been meaningless" (84), that the message Stillman seems to be sending to Quinn is purely arbitrary or not meant to be a message at all.

> (...) Stillman had not left his message anywhere. True, he had created the letters by the movement of his steps, but they had not been written down. It was like drawing a picture in the air with your finger. The image vanishes as you are making it. There is no result, no trace to mark what you have done. And yet, the pictures did exist--not in the streets where they had been drawn, but in Quinn's red notebook. He wondered if Stillman had sat down each night in his room and plotted his course for the following day or whether he had improvised as he had gone along. It was impossible to know (85/86).

The notion of plot as spelled out by Brooks, the mapping of the criminal's path is two-fold parodied in this sequence. If Stillman really sat down every night "to plot his course" and thus Quinn's, the whole meaning of a detective novel, in which the criminal (the author) 'unintentionally' leaves clues for the detective (or, if intentionally left, rather in the form of 'red herrings'; but not intentionally left *and* virtually invisible for the reader and the detective) would be undermined. Secondly, Quinn is uncertain whether Stillman "plotted or improvised" the course, which leaves us to think whether Auster plotted the story or improvised, if it is 'real' or just an illusion. This question then raises another, even more important question: is there a plot at all? And if yes, following Barthes, is there an enigma? After Quinn has mapped the third day of Stillman's walk, he pauses to think over his enterprise.

> Quinn paused for a moment to ponder what he was doing. Was he scribbling nonsense? Was he feeble-mindedly frittering away the evening, or was he trying to find something? Either response, he realized, was unacceptable. If he was simply killing time, why had he chosen such a painstaking way to do it? Was he so muddled that he had no longer the courage to think? On the other hand, if he was not merely diverting himself, what was he actually up to ? It seemed to him that he was looking for a sign. He was ransacking the chaos of Stillman's movements for some glimmer of cogency.

---

[182] Lavender, p. 231.

> This implied one thing: that he continued to disbelieve the arbitrariness of Stillman's actions. He wanted there to be a sense to them, no matter how obscure (83).

The new map, the new plot, seems to be the answer to the inadequacy of plot in a traditionally structured detective novel. When such a structure becomes unproductive, new experiments are tried. Quinn is looking for a sign to make sense of the 'plotting', to go on with the story. That, however, requires meaning and Quinn does not find a new way of orienting himself. The arbitrariness of the postmodern sign prevents him from solving the new enigma, the new question: Is there meaning? Auster's novel does not transmit that meaning, that kind of predictable, comfortable meaning provided by a traditional detective story. As Quinn starts "fiddling" with the letters, "switching them around, pulling them apart, rearranging the sequence" (85), he seems to resemble the randomness of plot, of events, of the story that could easily have developed differently.

What adds to the arbitrariness of the plot is that the sentence TOWER OF BABEL, that Quinn has formed to have the illusion of at least one meaning, is not finished. The last two days (or letters if you want) are never plotted and like the old man's message, Quinn's story remains incomplete, fragmentary, and unsatisfactory. Lavender writes that "the movement of the novel as a whole can be plotted as a series of (...) ellipses"[183] and refers to the 'erasing' of Stillman Jr., the disappearance of Stillman Sr., and finally Quinn's journey into, what we might call, infinite open-endedness. It is the irony of the postmodern text, that something so full of signs could at the same time be so empty. Or as Mireille Rosello puts it: "The fiction of the walking word remains a wild hypothesis, an unrewarded attempt."[184] By briefly turning our attention to G and TLR, it can be seen that CoG is not the only novel within the trilogy that is concerned with the postmodern deviation of plot.

---

[183] Lavender, p. 233.

[184] Mireille Rosello, "The Screener's Maps: Michel de Certeau's 'Wandersmänner' and Paul Auster's Hypertextual Detective", in: George P. Landow (ed.), *Hyper/Text/Theory* (Baltimore: John Hopkins University Press, 1994), p. 151.

5.6.2 Plot in *Ghosts*

In *Ghosts*, the notion of plot is, if we follow Brook's account, subverted from the very beginning because the story is not told in the past tense but in the narrative present. This gives the reader an awkward feeling of a story that cannot be re-told and gone over by the detective again, and thus cannot fulfill one characteristic feature of the genre as presented by Brooks, since it 'has never been told', since nothing has happened so far. All the events are yet to come, again strengthening the assumption of an improvised, incomplete text. The omniscient narrator tells us that "the present is no less dark than the past, and its mystery is equal to anything the future might hold. Such is the way of the world: one step at a time, one word and then the next" (162). Another problem for Blue is that Black does not seem to move, to do anything besides reading and writing, which makes it extremely difficult for Blue to map, to plot Black's action. Hence, the plot itself seems to be on a standstill, as one little sequence underlines. "This goes on for several hours, and Blue is none the wiser for his efforts. At six o' clock he writes the second sentence in his notebook: This goes on for several hours" (164). There is no crime, there seems to be no culprit, no criminal whom the detective may follow, in order to repeat his steps and formulate the story of crime, the *fabula*. Blue is "not used to sitting around like this, and with the darkness closing in on him now, it's beginning to get on his nerves. He likes to be up and about, moving from one place to another, doing things" (166). This lack of events causes a shift in the direction of the plot, leading Blue backwards into his past, his memory, and older cases. The whole case is characterised by a poor "visibility" for the reader and Blue himself, who "has trouble deciphering what is happening" (168). In the same way as "Black appears to be no more than a shadow" (168), the shape of the plot in G is a mere skeleton, stripped down to its bare bones. In CoG, Quinn is looking for a sign to find some meaning in his 'plotting' of Stillman, Blue rather

> begins to advance certain theories, (...) making up stories. (...) Day by day, the list of
> these stories grows, with Blue sometimes returning in his mind to an early story to add
> certain flourishes and details and at other times starting over again with something new.
> Murder plots, for instance, and kidnapping schemes for giant ransoms. As the days go
> on, Blue realizes there is no end to the stories he can tell. For Black is no more than a

kind of blankness, a hole in the texture of things, and one story can fill this hole as well as any other (173).

As there is "no end to the stories" Blue can tell, there will be no end to this story, which could develop in this or that direction. The direction does not seem to matter since the case, the process of detection and thus the plot itself does not allow for any retelling of the unpresent story of crime. "It goes on and on", and "there will never be any end to it" (222). "To knock on the door, to erase the whole story--it's no less absurd than anything else" (227). Auster denies causality, a coherent plot, and--in true 'Black-fashion'-- makes the reader aware of the grotesque question: "Why ask questions when you already know the answer?" (229). The answer is, that there is no answer, "for we know nothing" (232), and are not supposed to know more. In a postmodern detective novel a positivistic, ever-solving and coherent *Weltanschauung* has lost its meaning, its significance. Auster creates such postmodern insignificance and indifference by means of his treatment of plot in *Ghosts*.

5.6.3 Plot in *The Locked Room*

At first, *The Locked Room* seems to have little to offer with regard to the postmodern subversion of plot. Told in the narrative past by a first-person nameless narrator, the reader accompanies the detective as he goes over the "ground" his former friend Fanshawe has left for him. Auster seems to surprise the reader with a linear plot that comes close to the treatment of plot in realism, as the reader eagerly awaits the deciphering of the plot, which is supposed to be analogous with the detective's uncovering of the crime. Yet again, the reader's expectations are left unfulfilled and the lack of crime as well as the lack of a criminal brings into question the meaning of the detective's quest once more. Although TLR is obviously less a detective novel than its two predecessors, it still could be considered to be within the genre of postmodern detective fiction. This is based on the hypothesis that it is again a multi-layered text. This time it seems to be easier for the reader to follow the narrator and to comprehend his actions. However, he must find out that Fanshawe is never really 'present' in the story (if he is, then only through his writing), which makes it extremely difficult to 'read' Fanshawe's traces (in its two meanings, namely the condition of reading, as in 'reading a book' and the process of reading, of making sense of the plot). "Out of nowhere, Fanshawe had suddenly reappeared in my life. But no sooner was his name mentioned than he had vanished again" (236). The story is not characterised by the same minimalism as in G. Nevertheless, only a 'ghost' of plot, an indefinite, undefined structure is reflected in the 'ever-present' unpresence of Fanshawe and thus the narrator's blind quest for meaning seems to be floating through the entire story. Again, it should be noted that this is not visible on the surface of the novel, i.e. on the 'story-level', but rather on the more complex and thus less concrete level of perception. Perhaps this could best be described with the help of Fanshawe's 'box metaphor'.

> Fanshawe had always been generous in sharing his toys, but this box was off limits to me, and he never let me go in it. It was his secret place (...) and when he sat inside and closed it up around him, he could go wherever he wanted to be. But if another person ever entered his box, then its magic would be lost for good (260).

To enter the plot means at the same time to leave it forever. Like Fanshawe, the plot could go "wherever [it] wanted to be", but "another person" (for example the reader or the narrator) who tries to enter the plot would then only cause the plot to lose its magic. The narrator is desperately looking for some cogency in the plot "pushing buttons and pulling levers, scrambling from valve chambers to circuit boxes, adjusting a part here, devising an improvement there, listening to the contraption hum and chug and purr, oblivious to everything but the din of [his] brainchild" (273). Like an engineer, he works on the case, on the plot, in order to fit together what does not want to be pieced together. This is again reflected in the lack of closure, which is present in the whole trilogy. The reader has closely followed the detective in the third story and is reminded that, at least, there is determinacy in the fact that there is never any determinacy. "Stories without endings can do nothing but go on forever, and to be caught in one means that you must die before your part in it is played out" (278). We are left with the plot and the story incomplete, the narrator still alive but not any smarter than before. No crime, no culprit, no solution. To account for the postmodern deviation of plot in TLR, it cannot be expressed any better than with the following words of the nameless narrator: "For when anything can happen--that is the precise moment when words begin to fail" (355).

5.7 Concepts of Reading

After the above discussion of a variety of features concerned with the art of postmodern narrative discourse, including such concepts as text, writing, author(ity) and plot, there remains one important link between all these aspects mentioned above: the concept of reading. As discussed earlier, two basically separate stories exist in a detective novel, namely the story of crime (which consists of action) and the story of investigation (which is concerned with knowledge). In his essay on narrativity and reading concepts, Hühn argues that the author of the first story is the criminal, who then leaves traces for the detective (and reader) to decode these traces in the same way as the reader decodes the text. This has a lot to do with plot but also with the concept of reading and, as discussed later, with the postmodern deviation of reading concepts, combined with the lack of closure. The detective takes over the role of the author and writes the second text, the true version of the crime. Hühn describes the relation of these two stories as follows: "(...) The central contest acted out in all classical formula novels [is] the contest between author (criminal) and reader (detective) about the possession of the meaning of the (first) story."[185] In other words, the detective story reflects reading itself. In Auster's trilogy, meaning is frequently denied and "the reader is also engaged in a tail job, trying to solve puzzles of names, doubles and identities."[186] Freywald further points out that Auster has redefined a "structural concept of the detective novel: the reader has taken over the work of detection in the reading process, and the detective has become the one to observe."[187] She is, however, only partially correct in her thesis, as, what she reserves for Auster's stories, is already inherent within the classical detective story.[188] Yet, the readers of the trilogy are able to observe the detective on many levels, for Auster creates a multi-layered text, in which the readers lose their orientation. Who are all these multiple readers?

---

[185] Hühn, p. 459.

[186] Freywald, p. 150.

[187] Freywald, p. 150.

[188] This has already been stated by Anne M. Holzapfel in her book on Auster. The discrepancy in Freywald's article, however, is obvious as soon as one reads Hühn's essay in combination with Freywald's.

The reader may appear as the detective, the detective's chronicler and the real reader. The real reader can also be an author, because he creates his own text while trying to solve the case. In CoG, the real readers must fail alongside Quinn and Stillman, as they have to rely on an unreliable, incomplete second story, narrated only with the help of Quinn's red notebook, which in itself is anything but a reliable source. In Auster's detective fiction, the reader is not only the one who follows the detective, speculates about the case and then writes his own text. He is at the same time dependent upon the detective, as he "sees the world through the detective's eye," experiencing the proliferation of its details as if for the first time. If the reader is stripped of his possibility to compare his own text with that of the detective (for Quinn fails to come up with anything), he must also fail in his struggle for meaning and solution.

Like Quinn in CoG, Blue is a reader of clues, trying to make sense of Black's behavior, of his walks, of his writings. He watches Black constantly, follows him wherever he goes, always hoping for some useful evidence. Yet, like Quinn, he fails as a detective and reader. "Blue keeps looking for some pattern to emerge, for some clue to drop in his path that will lead him to Black's secret. But Blue is too honest a man to delude himself, and he knows that no rhyme or reason can be read into anything that's happened so far" (181/82). In his eager attempt to fulfill his duty, Blue follows Black into a bookstore and buys the same book (Thoreau's *Walden*), Black is reading at home. "If he can't read what Black writes, at least he can read what he reads" (181). But Blue also fails as a reader of literature, "he feels as though he was entering an alien world" (193). This failure is mostly due to the fact that he "has never read much of anything except newspapers and magazines, and an occasional adventure novel when he was a boy" (194). His experience with the book resembles the case. Things are not moving, and if they are moving at all, it is going too slow for Blue. In *Walden*, Blue seems to have found a hidden clue, which provides him with the knowledge he would need for the book and for the case: "In the third chapter he comes across a sentence that finally says something to him-- Books must be read as deliberately and reservedly as they were written--and suddenly he understands that the trick is to go slowly, more slowly than he has ever gone with the words before" (194). As it turns out, Blue has not learned his lesson because he keeps away from the book and ignores its richness in meaning. This proves to be his biggest mistake as he is unable to read his own story that lies within the book.

> What he does not know is that were he to find the patience to read the book in the spirit in which it asks to be read, his entire life would begin to change, and little by little he would come to a full understanding of his situation--that is to say, of Black, of White, of the case, of everything that concerns him (194).

Blue's failure to read on two different levels, on that of the case and on that of literature itself, reflects the real reader's failure to write their own interpretation of the text and read the story through Blue's eyes. If Blue fails, the reader has to fail along with him. This failure results in the lack of closure because the quest for meaning abruptly terminates with the death of Black. Anne Holzapfel seems to have an explanation for that, when she states that "Blue's attempts to read have to end with the death of the author Black. Blue is left alone with the text written by Black, i.e. his own story, and is unable to close the circle present on the novel's second level."[189]

The nameless narrator in TLR is also a reader of clues and a reader of literature, this time, however, the two levels are congruent, since Fanshawe's clues are only of literary, i.e. written nature, these being his letters to the narrator, his manuscripts, and, finally, the red notebook. As in the trilogy's other novels, the position of the third reader is taken over by the real readers. In order to be drawn into the circle of the trilogy's repetition, the nameless narrator is also doomed to fail in his position as reader, just like Quinn and Blue before him. He is unable to find Fanshawe until he receives a second letter, which directly leads him to Fanshawe's locked room. Fanshawe, then, leaves him the red notebook, in which he is supposed to find a solution for all his questions. Yet, as he is unable to understand the content of the notebook, he fails as literary reader. Without a solution, the real reader cannot close his own text and interpretation of the clues, and thus contributes to the indeterminacy and plurality of Auster's multi-layered postmodern texts. No one is able to "find the one path" that leads to a complete reading of TLR and the NYT in general.

> It was an infinitely hungry organism, and in the end I saw that there was nothing to prevent it from becoming as large as the world itself. (...) I was a detective, after all, and my job was to hunt for clues. faced with a million bits of random information, led down

---

[189] Holzapfel, p. 71.

a million paths of false inquiry, I had to find the one path that would take me where I wanted to go (332).

This "infinitely hungry organism" of postmodern deviation of text, writing, reading, plot and author(ity) could only have been examined by means of language, constituted by words. In the NYT, Auster is very much concerned with the aspect of language, its arbitrariness, the question how language constitutes our world, and how we are constituted by language. This shall be dealt with in the following chapter.

In the beginning was the word.
--Gospel of St. John--

6 Language: The New York Babel, or 'The Arbitrariness of the Postmodern Sign'

Auster's treatment of language in the NYT is invariably connected to the term logocentrism (from the Greek *logos*, word), coined by Derrida, which basically means 'centered on the word'. It also describes the form of metaphysics that understands writing as merely a representation of speech, and thus makes it secondary to speech, which is privileged because an utterance is present simultaneously to both speaker and listener. This situation seems to guarantee the transmission of meaning. Hence, writing can only be a weak copy of speech, the latter embodying and conveying presence and thus meaning. Deconstruction tries to undo this opposition between writing and speech to open up texts for an endless play of '*différance*', "the systematic play of differences, of the traces of differences, of the spacing by means of which elements are related to each other."[190] As a play of differences, language offers no basis for attributing a determinate meaning to any word or utterance. Our Western culture is organised around the belief or hope that there is meaning in language and even some ultimate final meaning, such as God or truth. Postmodernism in general and deconstruction in particular deny the belief of an ultimate and univocal truth inherent within language. "Language is not truth. It is the way we exist in the world. Playing with words is merely to examine the way the mind functions, to mirror a particle of the world as the mind perceives it."[191] Therefore, the return to pure *logos* is impossible. According to Derrida, there is no such thing as the 'Transcendental Signified': "The absence of a transcendental signified extends the domain and play of signification endlessly."[192] Language can never convey absolute meaning since none of us fully possesses the significance of the spoken words.

---

[190] Jacques Derrida, *Positions*, trans. Alan Bass (Chicago: University of Chicago Press, 1978), p. 27.

[191] Paul Auster, *The Invention of Solitude*, p. 161.

[192] Jacques Derrida, *Writing and Difference*, trans. Alan Bass (Chicago: University of Chicago Press, 1978), p. 280.

In his trilogy, Paul Auster denies the presence of language--which defines us as human beings--as a center in the world on which we can rely. "Language is never redeemed by the attendance ('and the Word was with God') or presence of an Author-God but rather is always already fallen, haunted by 'empty spaces'."[193] The arbitrariness of the postmodern sign is one reason for the de-centeredness of the characters in the NYT. Words cannot convey presence, reality or absolute truth. This has immediate impact on the form of the detective story, because centeredness is a function of motivation, which itself is one of the basic principles of the detective story. In the centered world of classical detective fiction, signs and clues are finally and fully motivated. Malmgren points out that "mystery unfolds in a pre-Saussurian world in which the relation between signifiers and signifieds is not arbitrary and not subject to the play of *différance*."[194] He refers to Poe's "The Murders in the Rue Morgue" and the scene in which Dupin deduces his companion's train of thought from his acts and gestures. By means of his postmodern detective fiction, Auster seems to bask in the indeterminacy of language, in which the signifiers begin to become detached from its signifieds. In referring to CoG, Chris Tysh raises the essential question, concerning the loss of meaning, the loss of truth in language itself: "What does one do with this obstinate business of tracing patterns, of looking for a way to harness that frightening mass of unmotivated signs into a recognisable shape, a grid by which to decipher something meaningful like a sentence or, better, a sacred origin?"[195] The answer is that none of the detectives and pursuers of clues in the trilogy succeed in combinig signifier and signified to a meaningful shape.

Due to the arbitrariness of the connection between signifier and signified, signs are only determined by conventions. These conventions refer the *concept* and the *image acoustique* (Ferdinand de Saussure) to our extra-linguistic reality. This process makes words human inventions that possess no essential ties to the things they name. Russell points out that "this quest for correspondence between signifier and signified is inextricably related to each protagonist's quest for origin and identity, for the self only exists insofar as language grants existence to it,"[196] which means, in

---

[193] Little, p. 141.
[194] Malmgren, p. 184.
[195] Chris Tysh, "From One Mirror to Another: The Rhetoric of Disaffiliation in *City of Glass*", *Review of Contemporary Fiction* 14:1, 1994, p. 47.
[196] Russell, p. 72.

a strict sense, that self *is* language. The fact that language, the arbitrary code which serves us for communicative actions, is unstable and its meaning indeterminate, "denies the self-exploring traveler access to an absolute origin, or self."[197] Language imposes its authority on the protagonists of the trilogy, who harbor the innate motivation of producing meaning through text. Yet, it is language that determinates *what* will be expressed. "If words followed, it was only because I had no choice but to accept them, to take them upon myself and go where they wanted me to go" (346). Martin Klepper underlines the important role of language in the trilogy.

> Die Suche nach der puren Sprache, einer Sprache, die keine Verkleidung, sondern absolute Transparenz wäre, die *prelapsarian speech*, in der Signifikant und Signifikat noch nicht getrennt sind, die also der postmodernen Indetermanenz, von der Hassan spricht, entgeht, spielt deshalb auch eine große Rolle in den Erzählungen. Solange sie nicht gefunden wird, d.h. solange die Sprache, die symbolische Ordnung (Lacan), dem Individuum vorgängig ist, wird Auster seine Inszenierungen immer wieder wiederholen müssen.[198]

Auster's obvious preoccupation with the notion of language in each of the trilogy's novels is the motivation for this paper to elaborate on this subject in this chapter. Russell states that "all three [novels] employ and deconstruct the conventional elements of the detective story, resulting in a recursive linguistic investigation of the nature, function, and meaning of language."[199] It is Auster's focus on language as constitutive of the self and the world that makes it so difficult for his characters to gain self-knowledge. As he places language between the self and the other (or world), he problematises their communication and thus their self-knowledge. When everything is text, then, the notion of autonomy (as we have seen in the last chapter) as a source for self-knowledge, is doubtful.

---

[197] Russell, p. 84.

[198] Klepper, p. 252. (The quest for a pure language, a language, that does not disguise itself but rather conveys absolute transparency, namely a prelapsarian speech, in which signifier and signified are not yet separated and which thus eludes the postmodern indeterminacy mentioned by Hassan, plays an impor-tant role in the stories. As long as this particular language cannot be found, i.e. as long as language, the symbolic order (Lacan), imposes authority on the individual, Auster will have to repeat his performances again and again [my translation]).

[199] Russell, p. 71.

6.1 Language in *City of Glass*

The title *City of Glass* evokes both "transparency, the vision of a city or language completely present to itself, and fragility, the vulnerability and potential shattering of a world in which transparency would be replaced by shimmering shards of broken glass. The title might thus suggest either a place where man may find his original, transparent language, or a place where man must learn to speak many different languages, where he can never be fully present to himself (...)."[200] The 'city of glass' denies transparent access to a transcendental signified.

Language in CoG has to do with the case and with the only crime that we are informed of in the novel. Peter Stillman Sr, a former university professor, had begun his career with a rather utopian project, namely the restoration of Adamic innocence by recreating language's prelapsarian original ability to reveal the essences of things and thus to convey meaning. His theory is presented in his dissertation *The Garden and the Tower: Early Visions of the New World*, which is divided into two parts, "The Myth of Paradise" and "The Myth of Babel". Although language and the search for the signifier to convey presence is a major preoccupation of all the novels in the trilogy, CoG perhaps presents this theme with the most force and clarity. By dedicating a whole chapter to Stillman's dissertation, Auster seems to make an important point, which is valid for all three novels and thus introduces the aspect of language at this early stage in the novel. Martin Klepper echoes this thought when he writes that

> Austers Text ist ein Experiment, das darin besteht, einen Roman zu schreiben, d.h. eine Sprache zu finden, in der die bezeichnenden Worte zu ihrem bezeichneten Gehalt zurückfinden, d.h. die Symbolisierung sich mit ihrem Wunschobjekt in der Wirklichkeit zu einer Einheit verbindet.[201]

This is the justification and evidence why Stillman's dissertation should be subject to a close examination.

---

[200] Pascalle-Anne Brault, "Translating the Impossible Debt: Paul Auster's *City of Glass*", *Critique* 39:3, 1998, p. 230f.

[201] Klepper, p. 255. (Auster's text is an experiment that consists in writing a novel, i.e. in finding a lan-guage, in which the signifying words can be traced back to their signified meaning, i.e. that the symbolisation is linked and united with its optative object in reality [my translation].

In the first part, Stillman claims that "the first men to visit America believed that they had accidentally found paradise, a second Garden of Eden. (...) Columbus wrote: 'For I believe that the earthly paradise lies here, which no one can enter except by God's leave.'" (50). This is the basis for Stillman's assumption that "America would become an ideal theocratic state, a veritable City of God" (51), in which he could execute his experiments to recreate the prelapsarian state of language, the tongue of the innocent Adam alone by which things can be reunited with their correct names.

In the second part of the dissertation, Stillman proposes a new theory of the fall in paradise. "Relying heavily on Milton and his account in *Paradise Lost*--as representing the orthodox Puritan position--Stillman claimed that it was only after the fall that human life as we know it came into being. For if there was no evil in the Garden, neither was there any good" (52). This ironic deconstructive reading of Milton's text results in Stillman's own quest for prelapsarian language. After having written his dissertation, Stillman criminally locked away his son and is now trying to free mankind from evil, that has been brought upon us after Adam's fall. By means of his second experiment in New York, he intends to reverse the pattern and do good instead of evil. The problem is that no one will ever be able to profit from his attempts, since he cannot find the signifier that conveys presence. Neither is he willing to reveal his 'new language'. During one of their meetings, Quinn asks Stillman for an example of the new language but Stillman declines: "I'm sorry, but that won't be possible. It's my secret, you understand" (94). Furthermore, he commits suicide and takes his secrets with him into his grave.

In his dissertation, Stillman especially dwells on the importance of the linguistic connection between knowledge and taste, again quoting Milton from his *Areopagitica*: "'It was out of the rind of one apple tasted that good and evil leapt forth into the world, like two twins cleaving together'" (52). Stillman shows how the word "'taste' was actually a reference to the Latin word 'sapere', which means both 'to taste' and 'to know' and therefore contains a subliminal reference to the tree of knowldge: the source of the apple whose taste brought forth knowledge into the world, which is to say good and evil" (52). Returning briefly to the real author Auster, we can trace back his interest in language and the connection of knowledge and 'food' to a time as early as 1974, when he wrote a critical essay on *Le Schizo et les Langues* by Louis Wolfson, in which he says that "speech is a strangeness, an anomaly, a biologically secondary function of the mouth, and myths about language are often linked to the idea of food. Adam is granted the power of naming the creatures of Paradise and is later expelled for having eaten of the Tree of Knowledge."[202] These thoughts by Auster forges the link to Stillman's view of language that he finds present in Milton's work.

> In *Paradise Lost* (...) each key word has two meanings--one before the fall and one after the fall. To illustrate his point, Stillman isolated several of those words--sinister, serpentine, delicious--and showed how their prelapsarian use was free of moral connotations, whereas their use after the fall was shaded, ambigious, informed by a knowledge of evil. Adam's one task in the Garden had been to invent language, to give each creature and thing its name. In that state of innocence, his tongue had gone straight to the quick of the world. His words had not merely been appended to the things he saw, they had revealed their essences, had literally brought them to life. A thing and its name were interchangeable. After the fall, this was no longer true. Names became detached from things; words devolved into a collection of arbitrary signs; language had been severed from God. The story of the Garden, therefore, records not only the fall of man, but the fall of language.

It is in the name of this lost innocence that Stillman, the archaic father, subjects his son to imprisonment. "He locked Peter in the apartment, covered up the windows, and kept him there for nine years" (31). "The father takes literally logocentrism's claim that the glassiness of language is negated when there exists the constant presence of a paternal figure, a speaking subject who acts as what Derrida calls 'the *father* of his speech'."[203] Stillman starves his son of contact with the outside world, isolating him from the drifts of words in order to recover the unbroken 'word'. The fall of language creates the postmodern fragmentation, indeterminacy and arbitrariness, on which the postmodern artist may create the essential void of *différance* and free-play. Auster's characters in CoG are helplessly trying to find a solid ground of meaning and presence conveyed through language and logocentrism. However, this proves to be a rather unstable and 'floating' ground.

Stillman also writes about a second story of language, "an exact recapitulation of what happened in the Garden--only expanded, made general in its significance for all mankind" (53), namely the well-known story and last incident of prehistory in the

---

[202] Paul Auster, "New York Babel", in: *The Art of Hunger* (Los Angeles: Sun and Moon Press, 1992), p. 33.
[203] Little, p. 158.

Bible, the Tower of Babel. This theme, as we know, is taken up again later as a collection of letters that Quinn 'reads' in Stillman's walks through New York. Perhaps the most important aspect of this account lies in the fact that, while building the tower, "the whole earth was of one language, and of one speech" (54). Only after God's punishment for mankind's striving after glory and perfection by means of building a tower that "symbolized the universality of [man's] power" (53), did the world lose its unifying god-like language.

Stillman's last chapter in his work is a discussion of the life of Henry Dark, who lived in Boston in the 17th century and was a secretary to Milton. According to Stillman, Dark published a pamphlet, *The New Babel*, which presented the case for the building of paradise in America. This triggers Stillman's interest and utopian experiment of "undoing the fall of language by striving to recreate the language that was spoken in Eden" (57). When Quinn takes on the identity of Henry Dark in his second meeting with Stillman, we learn that Stillman invented this character. "There never was any such person as Henry Dark. I made him up. He's an invention. (...) I needed him. I had certain ideas at that time that were too dangerous and controversial. So I pretended they had come from someone else" (96). America should be the place of the new Babel, the new paradise, in which one language and one speech would again enable the people to live in the innocence of the prelapsarian universe. According to Dark's calculations, 1960 marks the start for the rebuilding of the new Babel. Quinn suddenly remembers that "1960 was the year that Stillman had locked up his son" (59).

Stillman's theory provides us with the linguistic theme behind Auster's work, namely the arbitrariness of the postmodern sign. Thus, postlapsarian discourse has become a collection of arbitrary signs,

> for our words no longer correspond to the world. When things were whole, we felt confidence that our words could express them. But little by little these things have broken apart, shattered, collapsed into chaos. And yet our words have remained the same. They have not adapted themselves to the new reality. Hence, every time we try to speak of what we see, we speak falsely, distorting the very thing we are trying to represent. It's made a mess of everything. But words (...) are capable of change (92/93).

Stillman is convinced that Eden can only be revived by erasing our new language and recreating God's language, which was spoken in paradise. Klepper points out that this unambigious language can only be of a radical solipsistic nature.[204] It is as private as Quinn's entries into his notebook, as hermetically preserved and existent in Stillman's brain as Quinn's 'detective existence' is in Quinn's. In order to make the language of the unfallen man available again, he experiments on his young son and subjects him to nine years of isolated silence in a dark room. "An entire childhood spent in darkness, isolated from the world, with no human contact except an occasional beating" (31). It is his aim to heal the breach between speaker and word, subject and object, reality and imagination. Like Quinn, he is a detective, seeking a solution, trying to achieve a reliable reading of the world. Yet, his search is fruitless, since clues and results, signifiers and signified are meant to be unmatchable. The severe consequences, however, of Stillman's experiments are visible during the only appearance of Peter Stillman Jr. in the novel: A hardly comprehensible yet remarkable monologue, where the "pathology of his speech ironically enacts the principles of language and reality Stillman and Quinn fatally reject."[205] The monologue is alternatively told in third-person and first-person point of view, underlining Peter's marionette-like existence. Victim and puppet as he is, his 'innocent' language is far from any meaningful or coherent substance. Peter Stillman's self is even more unstable than Quinn's own. If the self is language and is dependent upon a world with an essential linguistic order, then, the only thing that Stillman Sr. has achieved, is the absolute disintegration of his son from the world. A human being is doomed to fail in a 'speechless' world. Peter is not able to produce a structured and coherent utterance but instead only meaningless and distorted scraps and palimpsests of language. "No questions please.(...) Yes. No. Thank you. (...) I am Peter Stillman. I say this of may own free will. That is not my real name. No. Of course, my mind is not all it should be" (18). He is condemned to live with his own words in an interior world and whether he makes use of this language or not, does not really make a difference to the outer world.

> You sit there and think: who is this person talking to me? What are these words coming from his mouth? I will tell you. Or else I will not tell you. (...) Peter kept the words inside him. All those days and months and years. (...) Peter can talk like people now. But he still has the other words in his head. They are God's language, and no one else can speak them. They cannot be translated. That is why Peter lives so close to God. That is why he is a famous poet (18/24).

[204] Klepper, p. 261.
[205] William McPheron, "Remaking Narrative", *Poetics Journal* 7, 1987, p. 140.

Peter himself embodies the arbitrariness of the connection between language and the world when he says that "this is what is called speaking. I believe that is the term. When words come out, fly into the air, live for a moment, and die" (19). Later in the novel Stillman Sr. echoes his son's words when he puns on Quinn's name, that "flies off in so many little directions at once" (90). The short-lived existence of words are linked with the short existence of Peter in the novel. When language dies, the self must die. After his monologue, Peter never makes another appearance in CoG. His split identity is expressed through the various names he gives himself. He is Mr Sad, Mr White, Mr Green, Peter Rabbit, Peter Nobody and perhaps Peter Stillman (cf. 21-23)."For now, I am Peter Stillman. That is not my real name. I cannot say who I will be tomorrow. Each day is new, and each day I am born again. I see hope everywhere, even in the dark, and when I die I will perhaps become God" (26). Each day a new postmodern sign is born, yet nobody knows what it will be tomorrow.

One part of Quinn's job is the constant surveillance of Stillman and he follows him assidously through the streets of New York as Stillman picks up objects seemingly at random. "What Stillman did on these walks, [however], remained something of a mystery to Quinn" (71). For Quinn, Stillman's behavior seems entirely arbitrary, the whole idea of motivation has been undermined. Even though "the meaning of these things continued to elude him" (71), he is not willing to give in so easily. Quinn's tracing of Stillman is also a search for a transcendental signified, a "quest for a 'still' point or inmutable Real beyond the glassy contingency of experience."[206] Desperate for some sort of a 'sign', in order to "disbelieve the arbitrariness of Stillman's actions" (83), Quinn finds out that Stillman takes letter-shaped walks, or more correctly, he needs to believe in their existence. He needs to "believe that [Stillman's] steps are actually to some purpose;" it is an "article of faith for him" (74), otherwise he might have "wondered if he had not embarked on a meaningless project" (73). When those steps go nowhere, "he takes that arbitrary sign [THE TOWER OF BABEL] and turns it into a 'natural' sign, an iconic sign with pictoral correspondence between signifier and signified."[207] As discussed before, these are signs (clues) that nobody but Quinn is able to read, because they exist only in his notebook. Whereas in Poe's *A. Gordon Pym*, the hieroglyphs that might be a

---

[206] Little, p. 157.
[207] Malmgren, p. 193.

form of the first tongue of Adam, although undecipherable, are visibly inscribed "on the inner wall of the chasm" (85), Stillman's hieroglyphs are inscribed in the air, or simply in Quinn's imagination. The paradox here is that Stillman, while searching for a one-to-one correspondence between names and things (which would be the original condition of the prelapsarian language), creates signfiers that nobody will be able to combine with its signified as one is unable to find the "floating signifiers". Holzapfel states that "Stillman writes, or rather walks, the signifiers into the subject, i.e. into New York City, trying to give it a symbolic unity."[208] Klepper adds the following argument:

> Auf der metafiktionalen Ebene drückt sich in Austers Romanen eben dieser doppelte Prozeß der Versprachlichung aus, der am besten an Hand von Lacans Theorie des Unbewußten erklärt werden kann. Es handelt sich um 'die Einschreibung des Signifikanten ins Subjekt, [und] d.h. die Adaption der symbolischen Ordnung durch das Individuum, seine Ausrichtung nach ihr, und die Effekte der Spaltung, die sie verursacht.' (Haselstein 85) Die *quests* in Austers Romanen sind immer auch *quests* nach der Einheit *vor dieser Spaltung* [his italics], eine 'melancholische Subjektivität', die auf die 'Einheit und Identität' aus ist (Haselstein 95).[209]

Stillman is trying to change the unchangeable condition of language in our world. "If a tree was not a tree, [Quinn] wondered what it really was" (43). Of course we all know that a tree is a tree (the concept of a tree), but every language has its own signified for a tree, which makes it impossible to fill the gap between signfier and signified and reach their univocal meaning and unity. "The world is in fragments (...). And it's my job to put it back together again. (...) Not only have we lost our sense of purpose, we have lost the language whereby we can speak of it" (91/2). It is the intention of the postmodern artist to place his aesthetics "in a neverland of fragments, a place of wordless things and thingless words" (87).

When Quinn approaches Stillman directly to find out the truth about his activities, we learn more about Stillman's interest in and analysis of language. For him, a thing is its function: when a thing (he uses the example of an "umbrella") ceases to perform its function, it is no longer that thing, no longer that word. Thus, a

---

[208] Holzapfel, p. 42.
[209] Klepper, p. 252. (The double process of *Versprachlichung*, which is best accounted for with the help of Lacan's theory of the 'Unconscious', is in Auster's novels presented on the metafictional level of the stories. Lacan's theory is concerned with the 'inscription of the signifier into the subject, which means at the same time the adaption of the symbolic order through the individual, his orientation towards it, and the effects of the splitting, which is caused by it.' The quests in Auster's novels are also always quests for this particular unity before this splitting, a 'melancholic subjectivity', which is interested in 'unity and identity' [my translation]).

broken umbrella, that used to serve as a 'rain-protective device' no longer fulfills its original function. For Stillman, "this is a serious error, the source of all our troubles" (93). Post-Adamic language "can no longer express the thing. It is imprecise; it is false; it hides the thing it is supposed to reveal" (94). Are we, then, to infer that the essence of things lies in their ability to exclusively serve one purpose? Or does it rather lie, as Nealon puts it, "in the primordial state of flux that precisely allows them to be taken up for this or that use"?[210] Obviously, in our world, the flux of language precisely names the essence of things and thus relegates the question of the function of a thing to a secondary and thus inferior level. The conclusion one has to draw from this is that Stillman has ultimately failed in his experiment, because he has "misunderstood the world's essence by conceiving of it univocally."[211] In "The Decisive Moment", an article on Charles Reznikoff's poetry, Auster formulates what he views as essential for writers and which at the same time adequately expresses what Stillman has strived for in vain, namely

> to penetrate the prehistory of matter, to find oneself exposed to a world in which language has not yet been invented. Seeing (...) always comes before speech. Each poetic utterance is an emanation of the eye, a transcription of the visible into the brute, undeciphered code of being. The act of writing, therefore, is not so much an ordering of the real as a discovery of it. It is a process by which one places onself between things and the names of things, a way of standing watch in this interval of silence and allowing things to be seen--as if for the first time--and henceforth to be given their names. The poet, who is the first man to be born, is also the last. He is Adam, but he is also the end of all generations: the mute heir of the builders of Babel. For it is he who must learn to speak from his eye--and cure himself of seeing with his mouth.[212]

Like his son, Peter Stillman Sr. disappears from the story in this case by committing suicide, leaving Quinn suddenly alone in the novel, another signifier that is detached from his signified. Like Stillman, he moves aimlessly through the city and sees "many things he had never noticed before" (126). He seems to understand what has brought Stillman to New York. The fragmented creatures and their language, which nobody can understand in this "most forlorn of places (...), served him as an endless source of material. (...) The brokenness is everywhere, the disarray is universal. (...) The broken people, the broken things, the broken thoughts" (94).

---

[210] Jeffrey T. Nealon, "Work of the Detective, Work of the Author: Paul Auster's *City of Glass*", *Modern Fiction Studies*, 42:1, 1996, p. 101.

[211] ibid, p. 102.

[212] Paul Auster, "The Decisive Moment", in: *The Art of Hunger* (Los Angeles: Sun and Moon Press, 1992), p. 35.

In a last attempt to make sense of the world and to flee from the disintegration and fragmentation of the case, Quinn moves into Peter Stillman Jr.'s room. In this 'locked room' he physically relives the prelinguistic isolation, the experiences and conditions of Peter's childhood. Is Quinn trying to become what Peter was? A symbol for the naked innocence, in which one may find God's language? Norma Rowen may have an answer when she writes that Quinn "divests himself of his clothing, making himself completely naked like the child just emerged, or about to emerge, from the womb," in order to "issue the language of unfallen man."[213] Yet in the Stillmans' apartment, indifference and indeterminacy (or "indetermanence" to use Hassan's compund term of indeterminacy and immanence[214]) remain with Quinn. "Night and day were no more than relative terms; they did not refer to an absolute condition" (152). Later on, however, we sense a certain change in Quinn's perception of writing and language. He seems to have mastered what Stillman Sr. has striven for so long. "All words are available to me now" (101), just like the ingenious Humpty Dumpty (an egg, "the purest embodiment of the human condition" [97]), the "philosopher of language" who (or better which) is convinced that "when [he] uses a word (...) it means just what [he] chooses it to mean--neither more nor less" (98).

Through language, Quinn becomes invisible and transparent and he simply disappears from the novel when he has filled the last page of his notebook with his words. His time is over, but he seems to have attained certain qualities that characterise him as one of Auster's poets that "speak from their eyes", which enables him to turn words into things, to make words part of the world. "He felt that his words had been severed from him, that now they were a part of the world at large, as real and specific as a stone, or a lake, or a flower" (156). Now language is free to name the invisible. Or in the words of Roman Jakobson:

> Poeticity is present when the word is felt as a word and not a mere presentation of the object being named or an outburst of emotion, when words and their composition, their meaning, their external and internal form, acquire a weight and value of their own instead of referring indifferently to reality.[215]

---

[213] Rowen, p. 231.

[214] Ihab Hassan, *The Postmodern Turn: Essays in Postmodern Theory and Culture* (Columbus: Ohio State University Press, 1987). "The arts of indetermanence (...) continually play between self-reflexiveness and self-surrender." (80)

[215] Roman Jakobson, "What is Poetry" (1934), quoted in: Peter Kirkegaard, "Cities, Signs and Meaning in Walter Benjamin and Paul Auster, or: never sure of any of it", *Orbis Litterarum* 48, 1993, p. 170.

Quinn witnesses the transformation of his own language, a reunification of words and things, of language and the world, a de-subjectivization of language. At the beginning of the novel, he felt that his words had become severed from him, since "he did not consider himself to be the author of what he wrote" (5), they were not his own words. Now, as "the case was far behind him" (156), he has left his triad of selves as the "two William Wilsons cancelled each other out" (153) and the words become severed from him due to the fact that he has rubbed himself out within them. "They no longer had anything to do with him" (156). As Norma Rowen puts it, Quinn "made his way back to language's unfallen core and gave it utterance. (...) [Yet], he was not able to come up with the correct text of reality, (...) he did not achieve any cosmic solution. (...) Quinn's contact with the pure prelapsarian word has been partial, momentary and personal."[216] In a last attempt to alter reality and to preserve the innocence of language, "he wondered if he had it in him to write without a pen, if he could learn to speak instead, filling the darkness with his voice, speaking the words into the air, into the walls, into the city, even if the light never came back again" (156/7). Quinn's wish is not granted. In the end, the world and the language in the Babel of New York is as fragmented, arbitrary, and fallen as it was at the beginning. What will happen with language when there are no more pages in the red notebook? Again, Auster leaves us without a final solution. Logocentrism, "the crime that Auster investigates"[217] deconstructs itself in CoG. To find a world, in which a language links signifier and signfied, Quinn and Auster, fiction and reality to a coherent unity, is a nostalgic dream. CoG rather underlines the postmodern impossibility of such a dream and at the same time the compulsion to start all over again with a new attempt of recreating this unity.[218]

6.2 Language in *Ghosts*

The notion of language in G is not as dominant as in CoG, but, as discussed earlier, of similar complexity and also marked by the detective's logocentric perception of language and the world. Like CoG, "the title of *Ghosts* suggests transparency, the

---

[216] Rowen, p. 232.
[217] Russell, p. 72.
[218] cf. also Klepper, p. 266.

ideal logocentric relationship between signifier and signified (...)."[219] To Blue, words are congruent with the objects they refer to. When his first report is due, the narrator allows us a glance into Blue's confidence about the words he uses and his method of writing.

> His method is to stick to outward facts, describing events as though each word tallied exactly with the thing described, and to question the matter no further. Words are transparent for him, great windows that stand between him and the world, and until now they have never impeded his view, have never even seemed to be there. Oh, there are moments when the glass gets a trifle smudged and Blue has to polish it in one spot or another, but once he finds the right word, everything clears up (174).

"Governed by the fantasy of matching signifier to signified, clue to crime, the stereotypical gumshoe is confident that signs conform to a classical economy of representation. Language, far from being marked by errancy, is characterised by glassy stillness."[220]

Blue's perception of language is based on his superficial view of the world and of his own life. "He has moved rapidly along the surface of things for as long as he can remember, fixing his attention on these surfaces only in order to perceive them, sizing up one and then passing on to the next, and he has always taken pleasure in the world as such, asking no more of things than that they be there" (171). Blue's obsession with the transparency and clarity of the world and his conception of it, is also expressed "in the primacy he gives to visual perception."[221] While attending a baseball game, he is "struck by the sharp clarity of the colors around him" (189) and he likes movies because "the pictures on the screen are somehow like the thoughts inside his head" (190). He suddenly becomes aware of a certain change within himself and of the world around him. The case develops in a different direction, being distinct from all the other cases Blue has worked on in his career. "Without being able to read what Black has written, everything is blank so far" (164). He has "trouble deciphering what is happening" (168) and complains about the lack of details. Language has become opaque to him and he begins to feel frustrated. He has to admit to himself that the facts relating to this case are scarce, which is mostly due to his inability of reading what Black is reading and writing. "(...) He is disappointed to find such paucity of detail. It's as though his words, instead of drawing out the

---

[219] Russell, p. 76.
[220] Little, p. 138.
[221] Russell, p. 77.

facts and making them sit palpably in the world, have induced them to disappear" (175). The ineffectiveness of language and his own accuracy of expressing truth and meaning through words drive him even deeper into doubts about himself and the case. "For the first time in his experience of writing reports, he discovers that words do not necessarily work, that it is possible for them to obscure the things they are trying to say" (176). As Santiago del Rey correctly indicates, "si se tambalean las palabras, también el mundo se tambalea."[222] Now, Blue has to take a different approach towards the case because the conventional methods of detection have failed.

> (...) It suddenly occurs to Blue that he can no longer depend on the old procedures. Clues, legwork, investigative routine--none of this is going to matter anymore. But then, when he tries to imagine what will replace these things, he gets nowhere. At this point, Blue can only surmise what the case is not. To say what it is, however, is completely beyond him (175).

Blue cannot come to terms with the case, his logocentric trust in language has failed him and he thinks about including fictitious stories in the reports, because "with so little else to report, these excursions into the make-believe would at least give some flavor of what has happened. But Blue brings himself up short, realizing that they have nothing really to do with Black" (175). Having abandoned this plan, Blue then brings himself to painstakingly compose the reports with his old accuracy. "But why does he feel so dissatisfied, so troubled by what he has written?" (176). His frustration results from the discrepancy between word and fact, between fiction and reality. He desperately tries to recreate reality by naming the objects in his room by the names he is used to giving them.

> Blue looks around the room and fixes his attention on various objects, one after the other. He sees the lamp and says to himself, lamp. He sees the bed and says to himself, bed. He sees the notebook and says to himself, notebook. It will not do to call the lamp a bed, he thinks, or the bed a lamp. No, these words fit snugly around the things they stand for, and the moment Blue speaks them, he feels a deep satisfaction, as though he has just proved the existence of the world (176).

However, Blue is mistaken in his attempt to reconstitute the unity of object, word and meaning. The world's existence and the arbitrariness of signifier and signified are two different levels, both being capable of 'living an independent life' next to each other.

---

[222] Santiago del Rey, "Paul Auster: Metamorfosis del Misterio", *Quimera* 90/91, 1989, p. 32. (If [the meaning of] words is 'shaking', then the world itself is also 'shaking' [my translation]).

For Blue, however, the one is irrevocably linked to the other. This conception of language and the world defines his dilemma. In Auster's postmodern detective stories, the aspect of language has consequences for the novel as such. To be able to solve the case, Blue has to rely on clues that are given to him by Black, which are present in his reading as well as in his writing. Since Blue fails in deciphering these clues and loses control over his 'fact-oriented' detective world, a circular structure with a satisfying solution cannot be achieved. In a way, language and its arbitrariness prevents Blue from successfully interpreting the case, the world and himself.

6.3 Language in *The Locked Room*

In the final story of the trilogy, the complexity and arbitrariness of language is again partly responsible for the detective's failure during the case. Here, the nameless narrator is forced to use that most dubious of instruments, that "clumsiest of tools, language, to ferret out what mere language can never discover,"[223] namely the essential presence of meaning in the world. Fanshawe is only present in the novel through his words, he is represented by language, by the signifiers, by the words in his novels, manuscripts, notebook letters and reports of friends and relatives. This is highly problematic, as we have seen in the other two novels, since language does not lead ultimately to the right solution for the detective. Yet, Quinn and Blue are at least able to confront Stillman and Black physically, whereas the nameless narrator has to rely on written evidence during his logocentric quest. Even at the end of the novel Auster leaves unclear whether the nameless narrator talks to the right person, Fanshawe. "'How can I know I'm talking to the right person?' 'You'll have to trust me. (...) I'm telling you that I'm the right person. That should be enough. You've come to the right place and I'm the right person'" (360). Uncertainty increases further when the narrator repeatedly addresses Fanshawe with his name and receives this response: "'Don't use that name, the voice said, more distinctly this time. 'I won't allow you to use that name'" (359). The narrator has to rely on words only and words are not enough to prove the truth. Schiff may have an answer for this when he states that

---

[223] Stephen Schiff, "Inward Gaze of a Private Eye", *New York Times Book Review*, January 4, 1987, p. 27.

"putting a name on something makes it at once available and all the more elusive, at once fixes it in front of us and obscures it forever."[224]

Fanshawe's words have an immediate impact on people who deal with his work. Stuart Green, the editor of Fanshawe's books says for example: "I read the book more than two weeks ago, and it's been with me ever since. I can't get it out of my head" (271). In the same way as the narrator feels a strong bondage to Fanshawe (cf. the chapter on identity), Fanshawe's words are a constant companion. This companion, however, proves to be highly unreliable because Fanshawe's words are "divorced from any context, which gives them a floating, disembodied quality" (322), so that the narrator has problems as to "fit all the pieces together" (288). The stable relationship of words and objects, signifier and signified is an illusion for both Fanshawe and the narrator. Only once does Fanshawe seem to be succesful in his efforts to gain control over his 'self' and the language he is struggling with as a writer. His solitary stay in the French countryhouse enables him to become another one of Auster's "eye-poets": "By now, Fanshawe's eye has become incredibly sharp, and one senses a new availability of words inside him, as though the distance between seeing and writing had been narrowed, the two acts now almost identical, part of a single, unbroken gesture" (326). Fanshawe had found another locked room for himself, in which he is almost able to convey presence through language. With the publication of his books, however, the door to his new room is opened again and the newly acquired language vanishes again.[225]

During his stay in Paris, the nameless narrator experiences a similar dilemma closely connected to language. Still on the search for some evidence that would lead him to Fanshawe, he almost dissipates into a silence and an isolation of the self that is marked by the inability to express himself.

> My French was neither good nor bad. I had enough to understand what people said to me, but speaking was difficult, and there were times when no words came to my lips, when I struggled to say even the simplest things. There was a certain pleasure in this, I believe--to experience language as a collection of sounds, to be forced to the surface of words where meanings vanish--but it was also quite wearing, and it had the effect of shutting me up in my thoughts (338/39).

---

[224] Schiff, p. 27.
[225] cf. also Holzapfel, p. 95.

Furthermore, he is forced to translate everything back into English and so understands only half of what is spoken. Russell points out that, since the narrator experiences language "as a collection of sounds", he "loses the ability to distinguish between signifiers and signified. (...) In place of stable meaning, he finds what Derrida calls 'free-play'. He becomes exhilarated by this freedom of language and his ability to name things at random."[226] He realises that "words were constantly failing [him] now" (340), that "apples are not oranges, peaches (...) not plums", as every word "was beginning to have the same taste" (342). While searching for the "real story inside the words" (292), he takes on the identity of the 'master of logos', who may name things at random and thus offers a possible solution to all his questions. He 'names' a girl in a bar Fayaway and himself Melville (347), perhaps comparing Captain Ahab's quest for the white whale with his own quest for Fanshawe. And then, out of the blue he seems to have found Fanshawe, although he perfectly knows that the person he has chosen can never possibly be Fanshawe. "If he's no one, then he must be Fanshawe" (348), and he shouts Fanshawe's name so long that it loses its meaning. "(...) My repetitions had gradually robbed the word of its meaning" (348). The narrator is the "sublime alchemist who could change the world at will. This man was Fanshawe because I said he was Fanshawe, and that was all there was to it" (348). 'Fanshawe', however claims to be called Peter Stillman, which is only commented by the still disbelieving narrator with the following statement that somehow speaks for the whole book: "Names aren't important, after all. What matters is that I know who you really are" (349). The arbitrariness of language, of the connection between word and object, name and identity is an ever-present concern in the trilogy and in postmodernism itself. "Stillman was not Fanshawe--I knew that. He was an arbitrary choice, totally innocent and blank. But that was the thing that thrilled me--the randomness of it, the vertigo of pure chance. It made no sense and because of that, it made all the sense in the world" (351).

Pure chance is "when anything can happen--and that is the precise moment when words begin to fail" (355). How words fail in their function to convey meaning can be seen at the end of the novel. In another locked room in Boston, Fanshawe has been working on the account of his disappearance. He eagerly fills the red notebook

---

[226] Russell, p. 81.

with information that will rid the world and the narrator of all doubts and rumours concerning Fanshawe's life and his actions. "It's all in the notebook. Whatever I managed to say now would only distort the truth" (368), he tells the narrator. Yet, the language of the text in the red notebook is beyond the comprehension of the narrator, or as Russell puts it, "the authority of logos is completely deconstructed."[227]

> If I say nothing about what I found there, it is because I understood very little. All the words were familiar to me, and yet they seemed to have been put together strangely, as though their final purpose was to cancel each other out. I can think of no other way to express it. Each sentence erased the sentence before it, each paragraph made the next paragraph impossible. It is odd, then, that the feeling that survives from this notebook is one of great lucidity. (...) He had answered the question by asking another question, and therefore everything remained open, unfinished, to be started gain (370).

Even though Fanshawe's words seem to possess great clarity and transparence, they cancel each other out and make it impossible for the narrator to understand the deeper meaning of the notebook. He seems to have no alternative other than to rid himself of the pages that were determined for him, as even these words are suspect. "One by one, I tore the pages from the notebook, crumpled them in my hand, and dropped them into a trash bin on the platform. I came to the last page just as the train was pulling out" (371).

However, one question (among all the others that will have to be left unanswered), one insoluble paradox remains: why has the narrator wasted so many words in telling the story in TLR, when, at the end, nothing comes of it? Maybe the answer is hidden in this statement of the narrator.

> If words followed, it was only because I had no choice but to accept them, to take them upon myself and go where they wanted me to go. But that does not necessarily make the words important. I have been struggling to say goodbye to something for a long time now, and this struggle is all that really matters. The story is not in the words; it's in the struggle (346).

If the story is not in the words, in the *logos*, but in the story, why all this "Derridean scepticism of the spoken or written word?"[228] Auster skillfully plays with our perception of language, as he drenches his novels with allusions to language, stresses the importance of the word, dwells on the obvious fragmentation of the world, which is due to the indeterminacy and arbitrariness of language, of signifier and signified. Does he want to say that, colloquially expressed, after all, 'language itself is not such

---

[227] Russell, p. 82.
[228] Freywald, p. 152.

a big deal'? Or, is language responsible for turning human existence into an immense struggle as it can never convey absolute meaning? It is the reader who has to make sense of the book and this is only possible through language. Auster is not willing to offer more than that.

This chapter on language concludes with a few appropriate words by Norma Rowen that might explain Auster's preoccupation with language in the NYT:

> Auster's reworking of the detective story as a quest for the definitive language finally tells us that it is not the correct and final text of reality but a text about the text that is the most appropriate one for the postmodern world. Stories about stories, books not of answers but of questions: these are the forms in which the difficult reality of our time finds its best embodiment.[229]

---

[229] Rowen, p. 233.

> Imagination does not invent the SOMETHING-NEW we too often attribute to it, but rather (...) imitates,copies, repeats, proliferates--plagiarizes in other words--what has always been there.
> --Raymond Federman--

7 Intertextuality, or the Text as a Case?--Paul Auster's 'Selected Highlights of American Literary History'

Auster's postmodern detective stories have all concealed literary sources and make allusions to other literary works, which, on the one hand, certainly enrich Auster's texts, but, on the other hand, can also be accounted for by yet another postmodern feature, namely intertextuality. This textual strategy, which we may provisionally define as reference to previous texts, has come to be understood as "the very trademark of postmodernism (...). Postmodernism and intertextuality are treated as synonymous these days."[230] As an American writer, Auster seems to feel obliged to base his work on the fundamental literary tradition of America that includes such authors as Melville, Poe, Hawthorne, Thoreau and Whitman. "Auster's novels are not 'auratic', they are fully aware of being artifacts, intertextual spin-offs, diligently referring back to a long tradition of storytelling."[231] This chapter, in order to gain a better understanding of the complexities of intertextuality, briefly considers its theoretical basis before it is discussed in the context of the NYT.

According to Ulrich Broich, intertextuality has been a general phenomenon in the literature of all ages. [232] Intertextual forms--which include quotation, translation, adaptation, imitation, parody and allusion--have been present in literature since antiquity. Renaissance and Baroque literature were among the most productive epochs concerning intertextuality. Authors of that age insisted on the normative value of the classics and their preoccupation with literature and its source in nature and thus used intertextuality to stress the fact that a poet can best imitate nature if he imitates the classics. Or in other words: "the more intertextual a poem is (...) the

---

[230] Manfred Pfister, "How Postmodern is Intertextuality?", in: Heinrich Plett (ed.), *Intertextuality* (New York: De Gruyter, 1991), p. 209.
[231] Kirkegaard, p. 175.
[232] Ulrich Broich, "Intertextuality", in: Hans Bertens and Douwe Fokkema (eds.), *International Postmodernism: Theory and Literary Practice* (Amsterdam: Benjamins, 1997), p. 249-255.

more strongly mimetic it will be."[233] Hence, intertextuality was then closely related to a mimetic concept of literature and the frequent citations and imitations of the Bible and other classical works served primarily to provide certain social and moral values. Broich offers a definition of this form of intertextuality and its communication process.

> An author refers to other texts within his own text expecting his readers to understand these references as part of the strategy of the text; and the ideal reader does not only understand these references, but is also aware of the fact that the author is aware of their presence within his text as well as of the reader's awareness of them.[234]

Thus, intertextual passages are clearly distinct from non-intertextual passages and it is considered to be different from both influence and plagiarism.

Postmodernist intertextuality, however, differs in various ways from intertextuality in the literature of previous ages and serves new functions. The term itself has been coined by postmodern critics and authors, to be precise by Julia Kristeva.[235] It was only later that the term was taken over by other literary critics, who mistrusted the postmodern movement and its wide concept of intertextuality and who were trying to account for older forms of this textual strategy. What exactly, then, is the postmodern concept of intertextuality? Julia Kristeva, a postmodern literary critic, claims in her book *Sèmeiotikè* that "every text is constructed as a mosaic of quotations, every text is an absorption and a transformation of another text. Thus the term 'intersubjectivity' is replaced by the term 'intertextuality', and the language of poetry has to be read, at the least, as double."[236] In *Roland Barthes par Roland Barthes*, the 'latter' writes, that every literary work may be characterised as a "chambre d'échos,"[237] in which the echoes of other literary works are endlessly reflected. Elsewhere he states that

> we know now that a text is not a line of words releasing a single 'theological' meaning (the 'message' of the Author-God) but a multi-dimensional space in which a variety of writings, none of them original, blend and clash. The text is a tissue of quotations drawn from the innumerable centres of culture.[238]

---

[233] Broich, p. 249.

[234] Ulrich Broich, "Ways of Marking Intertextuality", in: Jean Bessière (ed.), *Fiction-Texte-Narratologie-Genre*, Proceedings of the 11th Congress of the International Comparative Literature Association (New York: Lang, 1989), p. 120.

[235] cf. Broich, "Intertextuality", p. 250.

[236] Julia Kristeva, *Sèmeiotikè: Récherche pour une sémanalyse* (Paris: Seuil, 1969), p. 146.

[237] Roland Barthes, *Roland Barthes par Roland Barthes* (Paris: Seuil, 1975), p. 78.

[238] Roland Barthes, "The Death of the Author", *Image--Music--Text* (London: Fontana, 1977), p.146.

Gérard Genette's concept of the text as a "palimpsest"[239] provides us with a third image, and Harold Bloom sums up the definitions by claiming that "there are no texts but only relationships between texts."[240]

Although the above quotations differ in their radicalism, they all convey the implication that every text is intertextual in all its parts and that the distinction between intertextual and non-intertextual parts is irrelevant. A gradual development in radicalism can be seen, starting with Kristeva's image of one text to one pre-text, followed by Barthes' "echo chamber", in which Kristeva's implication of a mosaic-like perception, where fragments from other texts might still be distinguished, would no longer hold true, for innumerable texts intermingle, and ending with Bloom's concept that there are no texts at all, but only intertexts. According to Broich, it is only one more step towards the final radicalization of this concept of the text: "the assumption that the whole world is (inter-)text and that there is no 'reality' outside textuality."[241] This image of the world would correspond with Borges' "Library of Babel," the Universal Library, outside which there is nothing and in which we have the "certainty that everything has already been written."[242] In "The Literature of Exhaustion", John Barth has also commented on Borges' image of reality and logic in the world.

> The 'Library of Babel' houses every possible combination of alphabetical characters and spaces, and thus every possible book and statement, including your and my refutations and vindications, the history of the actual future, the history of every possible future and (...) the encyclopedia (...) of every imaginable other world.[243]

Hence, the distinction between original creation and plagiarism or imitation no longer holds true. Borges himself gives an example when he invents a writer named Pierre Menard, who copied the whole of *Don Quixote* word by word, thereby creating not a copy but an original work.[244] Now, the question arises which of the concepts of intertextuality mentioned above is employed by Auster in the trilogy? When Quinn scribbles "illegible palimpsests" (76), we immediately recall Génette's concept, and Kristeva's and Barthes' come close enough to Auster's concept. I would,

---

[239] Gérard Génette, *Palimpsestes: La littérature au second degré* (Paris: Seuil, 1982).
[240] Harold Bloom, *A Map of Misreading* (New York: Oxford University Press, 1975), p. 3.
[241] Broich, p. 251.
[242] Jorge Luis Borges, *Ficciones. Obras Completas 1923-1972* (Buenos Aires: Emecé Editores, 1974), p. 470.
[243] Barth, "The Literature of Exhaustion", p. 75.
[244] cf. Borges. pp. 444-450.

however, assert that Bloom's definition, although being the most radical among the above definitions, most adequately accounts for the notion of intertextuality in the trilogy. Auster even seems to take intertextuality a step further by referring, not only to other texts, but to his own texts within his own texts, thus constantly blurring fact and fiction (it has to be mentioned that this has also been done by other postmodern writers). Through this textual structure, the novels are held together, which also fits the narrator's confession in TLR, admitting that he is the author of the trilogy. A few examples shall illustrate the complex relation between the three novels.

The red notebook plays an important part in every story of the trilogy; Quinn circulates in TLR as a detective although he has already disappeared in CoG; there is Thoreau's book *Walden* in G, that provides the patronym of Dennis Walden in TLR; a Stillman who is no longer the Stillman appearing in CoG lends a fake identity to a Fanshawe who is not Fanshawe; Henry Dark, falsely historical in the first volume, is used by the actual Fanshawe as an alias while hiding in Boston; Mr Green occurs in CoG, only to reappear as Stuart Green and Roger Green in TLR; the colors that serve as names for the characters in G are mentioned again in TLR, during the narrator's job as census-taker; just like Blue in G, the narrator in TLR fails to contact his fiancée; Marco Polo's *Travels* is read by Quinn and the narrator in TLR is watching a movie about him; Columbus is mentioned in Peter Stillman's book, and New York's Columbus Square serves as a meeting place in G, as does Boston's Columbus Square in TLR; like Quinn, Fanshawe camps outside an apartment building; Peter Stillman Jr.'s physician is called Dr. Wyshnegradsky, who happened to know Fanshawe from his time in Paris; both Quinn and Blue are ardent walkers and share a fondness for detective stories; they also use disguises and pseudonyms for their encounters with Stillman and Black; Fanshawe's solitude in the country house in France and his description of nature remind the reader of Thoreau's *Walden*, which in turn is read by Black and Blue in G; and Quinn's encounters with Peter Stillman all take place around the area of Riverside Drive and the park, the same spot, where the narrator moves with his family. These are only a few intertextual signals that are sent from one volume to the next and I am confident that many more 'inter-references' can be found. However, let us turn back to Broich's examination of intertextuality in order to demonstrate that Auster's trilogy firmly stands in a postmodern tradition.

According to Broich, intertextuality is closely connected with other concepts, strategies and devices that have been regarded as typically postmodernist. Among those are 'The death of the Author', a literature of 'pla(y)giarism', fragmentation and syncretism, infinite regress, the end of mimesis and the self-referentiality of literature.[245] All these concepts have their place in the NYT, as discussed in earlier chapters. Postmodern literature no longer holds the "mirror up to nature" (Shakespeare, *Hamlet*) but can only mirror other texts and at the same time itself. Auster's use of the *mise-en-abyme* concepts in CoG and in G are good examples of that. In postmodern detective fiction, intertextuality generally has a deconstructive function. Auster's detective fiction does not want to fulfill the reader's genre expectations and he does not want to "stabilise the meaning of his text by making it appear as part of an accepted literary genre."[246] Tani has shown that postmodern detective literature tends instead to question the basic assumptions and deconstruct the conventions of this genre. The 'world' of the postmodern text, in which the characters live, does not mimetically imitate our 'real' world but a textual world which is an imitation of other texts, hence, of other worlds.

It is widely accepted among literary critics and scholars that postmodernism and intertextuality are two sides of the same coin. However, one important question with regard to the concept of intertextuality in the NYT remains: how can one account for the high frequency of intertextuality in a detective novel? What lurks behind Auster's motivation to blend fact and fiction, to embed 'inter-texts', to use small bits of his private life, and to dwell on his 'Selected Highlights of American Literary History? Is it not because he intends to draw the reader's attention away from the case he is confronted with in the story to a different form of mystery, when the text itself turns into a case for the reader? The stories break their frames to make fiction into a true 'investigation' for the reader. This simultaneously includes investigation into identity, writing, language, and literary history. The emancipation of the reader in a postmodern detective story in which he is forced to 'read' his own meaning from the text poses yet another problem: the unambiguous meaning of a text becomes blurred through intertextuality and thrusts the reader further into the postmodern void of endless clues built on presumably endless possibilities of textual

---

[245] Broich, p. 252.
[246] Broich, p. 253.

significance. Malcolm Bradbury maintains that "the reader, seeing through the eyes of the detective, shares his work of seeing significance everywhere--but is unable to give the offered world a plot or circumference, until certain orders have been discovered and certain deductions drawn."[247] As reader of detective fiction we expect meaningful readings and solutions and have to rely on what is written, i.e. on the text itself. Only if we solve the mystery of the text--our case--may we succeed in solving the mystery of the case within the story. This thought is somehow echoed by Priestman's answer to the question "what will follow if there are no more pages in the red notebook" (157); 'what is going to happen if all clues have turned out to be meaningless for the detective and the reader'?

> On one level, the stories suggest that there is no point in looking for ultimate meanings in essentially random experience, as the detective genre proposes; on another, it is a celebration of the kind of determination to find them nonetheless which characterizes both the obsessed private eye and the author, who similarly has no existence for the reader outside the necessary but doomed attempt to construct narrative meaning until there are no more pages.[248]

With these questions and assumptions in mind, this chapter casts some light on the hidden clues and open mysteries behind the following collection of intertextual bits and pieces, behind the inherent intertextual nature of the NYT.

7.1 Intertextuality in *City of Glass*

CoG covers many periods of European and American literature as well as historical events, persons, and connections to Auster himself. I consider it of great importance for the reader of the trilogy to decode Auster's allusions and references to writers and books, and of the interrelationships between characters within one story as well as on the level of the trilogy as a whole. Only after repeated readings of the trilogy can one discover these aspects and links, which is certainly part of the appeal of the book. Auster self-reflexively plays with this mixture of fact and fiction and guides the reader through a 'tour de littérature'. In CoG, Auster, the character, works on an essay on *Don Quixote* (cf. chapter 5.3 for a detailed examination) that seems to explain the

---

[247] Bradbury, "The Modern American Novel", p. 258.
[248] Martin Priestman, *Crime Fiction*, p. 65.

novel as whole. In this passage, autobiographical detail, historical fact, and pure invention self-consciously intersect. Dennis Barone stresses that Auster seemingly offers explanations but only to a certain degree. "Always Auster provides keys but we're never quite sure what door they open, or they might open a door for a moment of the key's articulation but then again, as it closes, all is lost."[249]

Edgar Allan Poe is one source to which Auster frequently alludes in the story. The link to Poe's short story "William Wilson" is visible in Quinn's pseudonym and in connection with the baseball player Mookie Wilson. William Wilson serves Quinn as a hiding place because all he knows from detective fiction "he had learned from books, films, and newspapers" (8) and a connection with Poe might clear his conscience of any doubts he might have. Yet, this is not only a reference to the 'inventor of the detective story', "it also corresponds with the disappearance of the self."[250] This is strengthened by Tani who writes that in Poe's "detective story-like tale 'William Wilson' the seeming solution destroys the solver."[251] Furthermore, Poe is quoted by Quinn in his notebook with the famous sentence from "The Purloined Letter": "And yet, what is ist that Dupin says in Poe? 'An identification of the reasoner's intellect with that of his opponent'" (48). The third reference is linked to Quinn's observation of Stillman. The discovery of Stillman walking words reminds him of "the concluding pages of *A. Gordon Pym*" (85). Here, Auster refers to Poe's tale "The Narrative of Arthur Gordon Pym", in which signs inscribed on rock play an important role. Freywald provides us with the hint that Poe is also connected to Quinn's surname. A man by the name of Arthur Hobson Quinn has written a biography of Poe, published in 1941.[252] Through some more investigation I found out that he has also edited *The Complete Poems and Stories of E.A. Poe* (1958). The following passage from CoG will perhaps serve as a proof.

> Once again, Stillman retreated to Riverside Park, this time to the edge of it, coming to rest on a knobby outcrop at 84th street known as Mount Tom. On this same spot, in the summers of 1843 and 1844, Edgar Allan Poe had spent many long hours gazing out at the Hudson. Quinn knew this because he had made it his business to know such things. As it turned out, he had often sat there himself (100).

---

[249] Barone, "Auster's Memory", p. 32.
[250] Holzapfel, p. 50.
[251] Tani, p. 51.
[252] cf. Freywald, p. 150.

Poe's contemporary Herman Melville is only once referred to in CoG, when Quinn is waiting for Stillman at Grand Central Station.

> He turned his attention to the photograph again and was relieved to find his thoughts wandering to the subject of whales, to the expeditions that had set out from Nantucket in the last century, to Melville and the opening pages of *Moby Dick*. From there his mind drifted off to the accounts he had read of Melville's last years--the taciturn old man working in the New York customs house, with no readers, forgotten by everyone. Then, suddenly with great clarity and precision, he saw Bartleby's window and the blank brick wall before him (63).

This passage contains two works by Melville, *Moby Dick* and "Bartleby the Scrivener", which intertextually exemplify two distinct features that are often present in CoG. One has to to do with frequent literary allusions to travelling and discoveries--which includes the basic activities of Quinn and Stillman, namely walking and 'discovering' evidence--the other one has to do with lonely, alienated, fragmented and de-centered characters, of which we find an abundance in CoG and the whole trilogy (Quinn, the two Stillmans, vagabonds and bums, to name only a few). *Moby Dick*, Marco Polo's *Travels*, Columbus, *Robinson Crusoe*, *The Journeys* of Cabeza de Vaca, Raleigh's *History of the World*, the Puritans on the Mayflower, Noah, and the 'I'-narrator, who has just "returned from [a] trip to Africa" (157) embody the group of travelers, whereas Bartleby, Kaspar Hauser, the children of Frederick II and James IV, Peter of Hanover, Alexander Selkirk (the ship-wrecked sailor who lived alone on an island), and Victor, the wild boy of Aveyron belong to the second group. Both groups seem to have one thing in common: they are all pilgrims, lonely wanderers, and explorers, who have to rely on language as their only source of meaning. The travelers claim unknown regions through language, as they have to give these places a name. The de-centered characters try to regain their ability to speak and write, as it is their only way of communicating with the world. Yet, both have to fail in their efforts. The travelers need to write down or tell their experiences in order to make them known for the world, and the speechless seekers remain in their isolation (cf. Peter Stillman, Kaspar Hauser, ...). Due to the arbitrariness and instability of language, no place can be completely claimed, and no language can be completely owned. Russell states that "as a travel narrative, *The New*

128

York Trilogy is nomadic in nature: the semantic journey never ends but consists of a never-ending loop of arrivals and departures."[253]

As a devoted reader of detective stories and through his own fictitious character Max Work, the third part of his triad of selves, Quinn constantly seeks to attain the attitude of the 'hard-boiled warrior', the detective prototype of Chandler and Hammet. In two passages, Auster seems to make an allusion to Chandler's Philip Marlowe. He plays the calm, detached, and convincing detective when he talks to Virginia Stillman about the case.

> Quinn smiled judiciously (...) 'Whatever I do or do not understand,' he said, 'is probably beside the point. You've hired me to do a job, and the sooner I get on with it the better. From what I gather, the case is urgent'. He was warming up now. Something told him that he had captured the right tone, and a sudden sense of pleasure surged through him (29).

Virginia Stillman is through her appearance also a typical female character of the hard-boiled genre: "The woman was thirty, perhaps thirty five; average height at best; hips a touch wide, or else voluptuous, depending on your point of view; dark hair, dark eyes, and a look in those eyes that was at once self-contained and vaguely seductive" (16). Quinn is immediately attracted to her and thinks about a possible love affair. The versed reader in detective stories might suppose that Virginia Stillman herself could be a possible culprit in the tradition of Chandler's Vivian Regan in *The Big Sleep*, but just like the two other Stillmans she vanishes from the scene without returning.

Auster seems to infiltrate his book with giants of American and European literature, that reach from Baudelaire ("Il me semble que je serais toujours bien là où je ne suis pas" [132]) to Beckett, whose play *Endgame* comes alive in the passage when Quinn decides to dedicate himself to a constant observation of the Stillman's apartment and hides near, under and finally in a dustbin. Actually, Quinn is indeed the most absurd character in the novel alongside Stillman Sr. In another context, Freywald points to a hidden allusion to Pynchon's novel *V.* from 1963. In the passage, in which Quinn's walk through New York is described, the reader is given a lot of details and geographical data about what at first seems an arbitrary and rather unimportant walk. Only a 'detective-reader' who follows Quinn's way will find out

---

[253] Russell, p. 84.

that he is walking the letter "V."[254] Auster takes the aspect of reader activity to its extremes, for only the most active and attentive reader is able to discover this hidden clue. The text turns into the case. In one of Quinn's meetings with Stillman Sr, more names of famous authors are woven into the text. Stillman mentions the initials H.D. when he explains to Quinn how he has come up with the name of his fictional character Henry Dark. Stillman talks Quinn into taking a few wild guesses, which result in a variety of illustrious people: Henry David, as in Henry David Thoreau; Heraclitus and Democritus; and Hilda Doolittle (97). The reader is probably most convinced by Quinn's last choice of Hilda Doolittle, because, as Marc Chénetier writes, "as a poet, she would not have denied the pertinence of a research concerning the links that exist between constellations and names (...) mentioned in *City of Glass*."[255] But, all wrong, the solution is (of course!) "Humpty Dumpy, (...) the egg" (97), a character from Lewis Carrol's *Through the Looking Glass*. As one is always tempted in a detective novel to make connections between any possible clues, it might not be surprising that Lewis Carroll is only a pseudonym for Charles Lutwidge Dodgson. So Auster's selection of intertextual references always seems to serve its purpose and differs from the characters' arbitrary actions. Stillman's dissertation is another good example of Auster's blending of fact and fiction that is based on some thorough research by the author. Actual historical figures like Columbus, Peter Martyr (alias Pietro Vermigli), Pope Paul III, Milton, Thomas More (the author of *Utopia*) , Gerónimo de Mendieta, Charles I, and biblical figures like Noah, Adam and Eve and God himself are included in Stillman's *The Garden and the Tower: Early Visions of the New World* that itself is a concised work of baffling coherence and mythical richness. Historical events and Milton's *Paradise Lost* are convincingly combined to offer a new thesis on the origin of language only then to be ironically subverted by including the fictitious character Henry Dark, a "private secretary to John Milton" (55), and allegedly the author of the pamphlet *The New Babel*.

The examination by this chapter of intertextuality in CoG concludes by comparing biographical data of the real Auster with the character Auster in the novel and with Quinn. Quinn is linked with the reality of Auster, who fictionalises himself twice: first, through the biographical parallels with Quinn and secondly, through his

---

[254] cf. Freywald, p. 153.
[255] Chénetier, p. 41.

appearance in the novel. The biographical data concerning Paul Auster is drawn from several interviews (mostly published in *The Art of Hunger*) and Volume 23 of the reference book *Contemporary Authors*.[256] A few examples illustrate the similar worlds of Auster and Quinn. Auster has scattered autobiographical hints in all three novels of the trilogy.

Quinn is "thirty-five years old" (3) in the novel, which is exactly how old Auster was when he wrote CoG. Around that time, Auster had been divorced from his first wife and temporarily lost custody for his son Daniel, which is Quinn's first name. Quinn also lost his wife and son, which is one of the reasons for taking on a pseudonym and writing detective novels. Auster also once wrote a detective novel under a pseudonym.[257] Furthermore, Auster often mentions the motivation behind writing CoG. He himself had received telephone calls in the middle of the night, in which the caller wanted to talk to the Pinkerton Agency. Of course, Quinn is drawn into the case through a call, originally intended for Paul Auster(!). Like Quinn, Auster wrote poems, articles, plays and mostly earned his money through translations at the beginning of his career. Yet, there are also striking similarities between the real Auster and the character Auster in the novel. When Quinn enters Auster's apartment, he is described as a "tall dark fellow in his mid thirties" (111), he writes essays (e.g. on *Don Quixote*), his wife bears the same name as the real Auster's second wife, Siri (Hustvedt), and the fictitious Auster's son Daniel bears the same name as Auster's son from his first marriage. Auster's family resembles the one Quinn lost five years ago and Quinn is painfully reminded of this fact: "He felt as though Auster was taunting him with the things he had lost, and he responded with envy and rage" (121). In the same way as Quinn's life corresponds with the life of the fictitious Auster, whose life then resembles the real Auster's life, do we find allusions to families, places, events and activities that concern the writer Paul Auster in the other novels. The nameless narrator in TLR 'inherits' a wife and a son from Fanshawe, and Black's apartment in *Ghosts* is in Brooklyn Heights, where Auster used to live after his marriage had broken up. However, this is illustrated in the following sections of this chapter.

---

[256] *Contemporary Authors*, New Revision Series, Vol 23, ed. by Deborah A. Straub (Detroit: Gale Research Company, 1988)

[257] Auster published the 'hard-boiled' detective novel "Squeeze Play" under the pseudonym Paul Benjamin. Later, he used this name again for one of the characters in the movie *Smoke*, for which he wrote the screen-play. In *Smoke*, Paul Benjamin happens to be a writer (!).

7.2 Intertextuality in *Ghosts*

In *Ghosts*, the most striking references and intertextual passages are related to such nineteenth-century Romantics as Thoreau, Melville, Whitman and Hawthorne. The most important work woven into this novel is Thoreau's *Walden* but there are also references to Hawthorne's "Wakefield", Melville's "Jimmy Rose" and Whitman's encounter with Hawthorne. All these references point to the major themes in G: solitude, loneliness, and self-scrutiny. The atmosphere of rest and solitude in Blue's and Black's apartments somehow resemble the loneliness and solitude of Walden Pond. Klepper also refers to the Romantic pretext, with which Auster underlies his postmodern cycle.[258] The equivalence of the two texts, *Walden and Ghosts*, is pointing to the fact that Blue involuntarily repeats what Thoreau managed quite deliberately: the retreat into solitude and self-reflexivity. Blue sees Black reading *Walden* and so he decides to read it as well. Yet, as we already know, he is disappointed by the book, which he considers to be "no more than a blather" (194). He is, however, in good company, since the narrator tells us that Thoreau's friend Ralph Waldo Emerson "once wrote in his journal that reading Thoreau made him feel nervous and wretched" (194). Solitude has helped Thoreau to breach the gap between reading 'nature' and gathering facts that would eventually reveal some truth in the world. Blue tries to read the case and actually finds some traces in the book that seem to resemble his own life and the case. One of the passages from Walden reads as follows: "We are not where we are (...) but in a false position. Through an infirmity of our natures, we suppose a case, and put ourselves into it, and hence are in two cases at the same time, and it is doubly difficult to get out" (200). Blue finally turns away from the only source that would have offered him some clues about the case and his life. But reading the book has at least helped him to gain some understanding of his situation.

When Blue finally musters the courage to approach Black directly he disguises himself "as an old man who used to beg on the corners of his neighborhood when he was a boy--a local character by the name of Jimmy Rose" (203). Here,

---

[258] cf. Klepper, p. 274.

Auster makes an allusion to Herman Melville's story "Jimmy Rose". However, as Eberhard Alsen correctly points out, this allusion functions differently from the *Walden* references because only Black, who is a versed reader in American Romantic literature [which might be deduced from the fact that he has "a bookcase on the north wall (...): Walden, Leaves of Grass, Twice-Told Tales, a few others" (219)], is conscious of them. Auster's choice of Blue's disguise involves two coincidences. As Blue is not a well-read person, he cannot possibly know that the old man's name is identical with the title character of a Melville short story. Secondly, Blue's disguise reminds Black of the poet Walt Whitman: "Has anyone ever told you that you look just like Walt Whitman?" (205). When Black realises that Blue is not familiar with the name Whitman, he tells him that "Walt Whitman used to work on this street. He printed his first book right here, not far from where we're standing" (205). Black then tells Blue two anecdotes about Whitman. One about Whitman donating his brain to a research team--accordingly, Whitman was interested in phrenology (perhaps also another reference to Poe's "The Murders in the Rue Morgue")--and having them perform an autopsy to "find out if there was anything special" (206). Unfortunately, an assistant drops it and it breaks. So, "the brain of America's greatest poet got swept up and thrown out with the garbage" (206). The second anecdote is about the time Thoreau came to visit Whitman. They discuss their views of life over a chamber pot full of excrement, which leads Black into a comparison with Whitman's brain, "the bumps and convolutions (...). There is a definite connection. Brains and guts, the insides of a man" (208). From this, Black then draws the conclusion that even the giants of the past--to those already mentioned they add Dickens, Henry Ward Beecher, and Abraham Lincoln--have become "ghosts" (207) and that anecdotes and stories *about* them are more interesting and valuable than the stories they wrote. "We always talk about trying to get inside a writer and to understand his work better. But when you get right down to it, there's not much to find in there--at least not much that's different from what you'd find in anyone else" (208). Hence, a writer is no more than just another ordinary person, his life and his thoughts do not make a difference to the world. This harsh critique and brute resentment of literature and its significance for us human beings again playfully lifts Auster's work onto a metafictional level. "Writing is a solitary business. It takes over your life. In some sense, a writer has no life of his own. Even when he's there, he's not really there" (209). As Freywald puts it, "*Ghosts* demythologizes the traditional image of the creative writer."[259]

From Whitman, the conversation moves on to Nathaniel Hawthorne, whose life, and whose short story "Wakefield" are two more important references in *Ghosts*. Black reports that after Hawthorne graduated from college, "he went back home to his mother's house in Salem, shut himself up in his room, and didn't come out for twelve years" (208). This clearly reflects Blue's and Black's self-imposed isolation which is further explained in Black's account of "Wakefield", a story, in which a man willfully leaves his home and family, only to spy upon them from nearby and to return after 20 years just as if nothing had happened in between. Just like Wakefield, "another ghost" (209), Blue leaves his partner and does not return for a long time.[260] In a way, *Walden*, "Jimmy Rose" and "Wakefield" are all stories that resemble the situation, in which Blue and Black find themselves in *Ghosts*. The only difference lies in the fact that both Blue and Black cause grief to the people they love. With this aspect in mind, "Wakefield" works best in comparison with *Ghosts*. When the conversation between the two is finally over and the two men say good-bye to each other, Black shakes Blue's hand and says: "My name is Black," (...) and Blue says, "Mine is Jimmy, (...) Jimmy Rose", and Black responds: "God bless you, Jimmy Rose" (210). According to Alsen, this "phrase echoes the refrain in Melville's short story: 'Poor, poor Jimmy--God guard us all--poor Jimmy Rose' (Melville, 246, 249, 251, 253).[261]" As Auster piles text upon text, story upon story, the 'text' itself becomes detached from the actual mystery and unfolds into a separate case for the reader. A few more examples of Auster's 'text-piling', mostly provided by Freywald, show what unexpected dimensions can arise from this technique.

To take his mind off the case for a while, Blue occasionally goes out to a bar, where he becomes involved with "a blowsy tart named Violet" and "gets her tipsy enough to get invited back to her place around the corner" (190). His own solitude and the 'danger' of detective work offer him an easy excuse for justifying his

---

[259] Freywald, p. 159.
[260] The same happens to Quinn in CoG and the nameless narrator in TLR. In all three stories the absence from home and the willful isolation is connected with the search for identity and meaning.
[261] Eberhard Alsen, "Paul Auster's *Ghosts* and *Mr. Vertigo*: Homage to the Romantics", p. 243.

behavior: "His guilt towards the future Mrs. Blue is scant, however, for he justifies these sessions with Violet by comparing herself to a soldier at war in another country. Every man needs a little comfort, especially when his number could be up tomorrow" (190). This is when Freywald joins the picture and detects a hidden allusion in the words "into another country". "It is Hemingway's Nick Adams story "In Another Country", which was incorporated later into *A Farewell to Arms* as part of Frederic Henry's story. The title of the short story in turn was taken from Christopher Marlowe's play *The Jew of Malta* (...)."[262] From Christopher Marlowe it is not far-fetched to make a connection to Raymond Chandler's detective Philip Marlowe, which then leads back to Blue, also a detective. So, does the novel for once close a 'postmodern circle'? Not at all. Apart from the fact, that Freywald's connections seem to be a little far-fetched, hardly any reader will find these hidden clues. This creation of many layers of texts does, however, explain what Barry Lewis considers to be Auster's dynamics of fiction: "his stories are built out of other stories"[263], which demonstrates that intertextuality is an important feature in the trilogy. Marlowe's play, Hemingway's short story and novel, Auster's text, and the reader's interpretation of the text build a "chambre d'échos" of five texts, each influencing the other. Thus, the conventional detective story, which usually consists of only two stories (cf. chapter 1 and 5) is expanded into a postmodern plurality of infinite stories and never-ending possibilities. The consequences of this development are chaos and disorder that prevent the detective and the reader from solving the case. This anxiety and chaos is expressed in Blue's feeling of multiple 'Blacks'.

> Two, three, four look-alikes who play the role of Black for Blue's benefit, each one putting in his alloted time and then going back to the comforts of hearth and home. But this is a thought too monstrous for Blue to contemplate for very long. Months go by, and at last he says himself out loud: I can't breathe anymore. This is the end. I'm dying (203).

We learn at the end that Blue is not dying but instead kills his shadow Black in a fight of two 'ghost doubles', which marks another intertextual reference to Poe's "William Wilson", as already referred to earlier.[264] Two final allusions to other literary models concerning the end of the story are mentioned by Freywald. She

---

[262] Freywald, p. 154.

[263] Lewis, p. 59.

[264] According to Freywald, the passage in *Ghosts* also includes the symbolic mask and the whisper in Poe's story (cf. p. 156).

writes that, apart from the allusion to Poe, the fight between Blue and Black resembles Bernhard Malamud's story *The Tenants*, in which a black and a white writer kill each other, "while the seemingly endless repetition of the word 'mercy' in the last lines suggests the interminable going on in the text without even a period to stop it."[265] Another Malamud context is established by a reference to his novel *A New Life*, in which the protagonist is boarding a train in the East and "going West to start a new life" (232 *Ghosts*). Through further investigation one would most likely find more references to American literature, which constitutes one level of *Ghosts*. The second level consists of the uncountable stories that are yet to be told out of the infinite "Library of Babel."

7.3 Intertextuality in *The Locked Room*

TLR offers many autobiographical clues about the real author Paul Auster and alludes to famous works of American literature written by the Romantic 'ghosts' Melville, Poe, and Hawthorne. The latter is the most important literary source because the name Fanshawe is borrowd from the first book of this romancer. Arthur Saltzman has investigated this field and his conclusion is worth quoting.

> Auster's debt to Hawthorne is even more overt in this novel. *Fanshawe* (1828) was Hawthorne's apprenticeship Gothic Romance about a remarkable but doomed scholar who disconnects from the world and decays in solitude, while one Edward Walcott, who accepts life's ordinary involvements, earns life's fruits--most notably, the hand of Ellen Langton, who becomes his default. That Auster christens his heroine Sophie, thereby recalling the name of Hawthorne's own wife, plays further upon the autobiographical nature of Fanshawe's destructive allure for Hawthorne, whose tendency toward remoteness, both in his private life and as a recurrent theme in his writing, is well known. Intriguingly, too, Hawthorne and his wife labored together to keep the authorship of this less-than-accomplished first novel a secret, once again prefiguring, albeit with different aims, the narrator's conspiracy with *his* Sophie in *The Locked Room.*[266]

Like Auster's book, Hawthorne's is one about the quest for identity, about escape, pursuit, frustration with his own literary work and disappearance. Hawthorne, as Auster himself said in an interview, "turned against his novel in revulsion and tried to

---

[265] Freywald, p. 157.
[266] Arthur Saltzman, *Designs of Darkness*, p. 68.

destroy every copy he could get his hands on."[267] This is mirrored in the narrator's destructive act at the end of the novel, when he "tore the pages from the notebook" (371). And yet, Auster's and Hawthorne's novels both reappear, the former through the narrator's telling of the story, the latter by means of Hawthorne's inability to destroy every copy that was still available. "Fortunately, a few of them survived," says Auster in *The Art of Hunger*.[268] Auster's TLR again repeats the "Wakefield" motif, as Fanshawe, like Quinn and Blue, distances himself from his former life and abandons his family and his profession as a writer. The narrator's situation remains doubtful, since we are not told whether he returns to his family or not.

As for Melville, he is everywhere: first he is present in one of Fanshawe's letters to his sister, which begins with the ironic words "'Call me Redburn'" (321), a mixed allusion to the first sentence of *Moby Dick* (Call me Ishmael) and to the protagonist of Melville's novel, *Redburn: His First Voyage*; second, and this has been pointed out by Chénetier, "the recurrent use of the 'let's suppose,' or 'let's say' which, under the invocation of Ishmael, the wanderer, factorizes uncertainty"[269]; third, in the Paris bar, when the narrator fictionalises himself by taking on a new role as an author, instead of the one as detective: "The name's Melville. Herman Melville. Perhaps you've read some of my books" (349), he introduces himself to Peter Stillman. Let us also not forget the narrator's insistence on calling the girl in the bar "Fayaway, telling her that she was an exile from Typee and that I was Herman Melville, an American sailor who had come to New York to rescue her" (347); and, finally, because of the "obstinate walls on which characters more than a little reminiscent of Bartleby attempt, as full-fledged scriveners themselves, to read or inscribe the signs of their identity and of their obscure desire."[270] Freywald also mentions that an image of Melville's character Billy Budd is present in Fanshawe's letters.[271] The names Budd and Starbuck are mentioned during the narrator's account of his job as a census-taker (294). A last allusion to Melville is made during the final encounter between Fanshawe and the narrator. Fanshawe has locked himself in and

---

[267] Auster, *The Art of Hunger*, p. 264.

[268] ibid, p. 264.

[269] Chénetier, "Paul Auster's Pseudonymous World", p. 40

[270] Chénetier, p. 40.

[271] cf. Freywald, p. 153.

threatens to shoot his friend through the door, which is exactly what the title character does to the narrator in Melville's story "Jimmy Rose".

Edgar Allan Poe is, of course, also present in the last story of the NYT. "Poe and Stevenson were [Fanshawe's] models and had inspired him to write Gothic mystery stories and a detective story in the sixth grade" (252/3). Additionally, Poe's short story *The Pit and the Pendulum*, in which a man is held prisoner in a dark pit, exposed to all sorts of tortures, both mentally and physically, serves as a comparison to the anecdote about Peter Freuchen, which the narrator finds in one of Fanshawe's notebooks. Due to some fierce weather conditions, the famous Arctic explorer had to build an igloo, which caused the problem that "his breath was literally freezing to the walls, and with each breath the walls became that much thicker, the igloo became that much smaller, until eventually there was almost no room left for his body" (300). The difference to Poe's story, in which the walls of the pit, steaming from the heat, are closing in on the helpless prisoner, is that in the case of Freuchen, the man himself "is the agent of his own destruction, and further, the instrument of that destruction is the very thing he needs to keep himself alive" (300). This demonstrates clearly Auster's technique of using other stories' morals, implications and meanings to create his own philosophical stories that are woven into the novel. The Freuchen anecdote also characterises Fanshawe who "needed more breathing room than most men" (238).

Finally, Paul Auster again alludes to himself in the novel by giving his characters autobiographical features, which enable him to cross the boundaries between fact and fiction, between the outer reality of the world and the inner 'reality' of the text. This metafictional doubling is another of Auster's postmodern devices present throughout the whole trilogy. Like the narrator, Auster studied English and Comparative Literature at Columbia University (297), wrote literary reviews and articles (235) and worked as census-taker in New York (292). Furthermore, the narrator and Sophie name their new-born son Paul, born on "February 23, 1981" (354), which coincides with the day Paul Auster met his second wife Siri Hustvedt and marks the 'new birthday' of the real Paul. Like Fanshawe, Auster worked as a switchboard operator in the "New York Times" Paris office (324), as a caretaker in a cottage in France (326) and on a ship (319). An edition of Fanshawe's poems also bears the same title as an edition of selected poems and essays by Auster, *Ground Work* (cf. 327).

Through intertextuality, the blending of fact and fiction, and autobiographical features that are woven into the books, Paul Auster self-reflexively deals with his own writing and lifts his postmodern texts onto a metafictional level, always aware of the postmodern dictum that there are not texts but only inter-texts and that every text develops out of a text that has already been there. His stories are stories made of other stories. Auster's fiction is a fiction of little stories and anecdotes that continuously interrupt the common linear flow of the classical detective story and lead the reader away from the mystery of the case to the mystery of the text itself. The unravelling work of the detective within the story mirrors and assists the work of the reader, as both try to piece together the disparate signs that might eventually solve the mystery. "The reader of the detective novel comes metafictionally to identify with the detective, as both the reader and the detective are bound up in the metaphysical or epistemological work of interpretation (...)."[272] The fact that

> Auster's detectives are artificial, literary characters, identifiable only through their literary counterparts, a mix of double and triple identities from fact and fiction (Quinn), metaphors of split personalities and symbols of the contemporary writer's dilemma (Blue), or autobiographical *personae* or masks of the author, who is himself no longer to be relied upon as the last authority of his books[273]

does not facilitate the reader's task of interpreting the text(s). Auster's postmodern detective fiction is fiction which detects. He is conscious of his postmodern literary 'fathers' and of the fact that "in the multiplicity of writing, everything is to be *disentangled*, nothing *deciphered*; (...) writing ceaselessly posits meaning ceaselessly to evaporate it, carrying out a systematic exemption of meaning."[274] The lack of deciphering and the constant quest to disentangle the multiple presence of fragmented clues, creates the perfect ground for Auster's deconstruction and subversion of the classical detective novel. Meaning could be nowhere and everywhere at the same time.

---

[272] Nealon, p. 92.
[273] Freywald, p. 158.
[274] Barthes, "The Death of the Author", p. 147.

It is only in this way that we will be able to
discover his book for what it is: one of those
rare works that can change our perception of
the world.
--Paul Auster--

8 Conclusion

The central thesis of this paper is that Paul Auster's *New York Trilogy* is firmly
within the genre of postmodern detective fiction. A historical overview of the
different categories and forms of detective fiction--the classical, the hard-boiled, and
the anti-detective novel--has provided a theoretical basis for the discussion of
Auster's postmodern stories and how they deviate from their predecessors. Paul
Auster has self-consciously interwoven the concepts of truth and meaning, identity,
author(ity), language, and intertextuality into his work to investigate himself and the
nature and origin of the genre he is using. In each novel, Auster creates a surface
mystery that is soon relegated to an inferior level as deeper mysteries unfold for the
detective and the reader. The original features of the detective novel seem to remain
intact but are only used by Auster to dwell upon the complex nature of the deeper
mysteries. He raises certain expectations in the reader in such a way that the reader
believes to be confronted with a familiar classical detective story. Yet, these
expectations are left unfulfilled. He has chosen the detective genre as vehicle for the
postmodern themes, which are mentioned in this discussion. The reader is invited to
participate in the search for postmodern clues and interpret what he thinks is the
meaning of the text.

All discussed aspects point to the same principle--that of indeterminacy,
which manifests itself through frequent doublings, mirror images and open-ended
endings. The detectives in the NYT, their place in the world, and the world(s) as such
differ from the classical detective story and go beyond the realism of the hard-boiled
genre. In Auster's fiction, characters are developed and motivated to a much greater
extent than during the classical and the hard-boiled times of the detective story, in
which the action and the case were more important. However, in his postmodern
detective stories, the realist's image of that "old stable ego of the character" (D. H.

Lawrence) as a viable entitity, has been superseded by a de-centered, fragmented, alienated, and displaced subject. Raymond Federman heralds his version of the postmodern character: "The creatures of the new fiction will be as changeable, as unstable, as illusory, as nameless, as unnamable, as fraudulent, as unpredictable as the discourse that makes them."[275]

The confrontation between the novels' fictional world(s) and the 'real' world(s) creates a place for the detective, that lacks order, stability, continuity, necessity, and coherence. Auster's characters are constantly searching for their lost self, for the 'Other', the lost father figure that reveals itself as the meaningful and long lost part of the detectives' self. Layers of overlapping worlds and fluid settings produce a postmodern void, an ambiguity of persons and events, and multiple possibilities, in which the destabilised writer-detective can only get lost. The rationality, logic, and positivism that mark the classical detective story, and the realism, inherent within the hard-boiled fiction, are not features of Auster's stories anymore. His novels merely unfold to expose more 'folds'. He admits accidents and gaps, loose and dead ends, he withholds information and refuses to reward the reader with a satisfying closure. The lack of closure reflects the fluid postmodern nature of the whole story.

> Whereas the puzzles posed by conventional detective novels are recontextualized at some delayed, yet dependable, last-minute appointment in the story, anti-epiphanic examples of the genre dwell upon the linguistic foundation of knowledge and remain as suspicious of solutions as of the problems that occasion them.[276]

The quest for identity is directly linked with the notion of a postmodern fragmented world. Many of Auster's characters show multiple identities, take on pseudonyms and see themselves reflected in their 'double'. In the course of the novels, originally split and unstable characters remain in the same condition, whereas formerly stable characters undergo the process of splitting during the search for identity. The recurrent theme of doubling, the fictionalisation of the characters, and the detectives' search that turns inward towards the self instead of outwards towards the case, make matters even worse for the reader, who is trying to read the multiple texts and, in

---

[275] Raymond Federman, "Surfiction--Four Propositions in Form of an Introduction", in: Raymond Federman (ed.), *Surfiction: Fiction Now...and Tomorrow* (Chicago: Swallow, 1981), p. 12.
[276] Saltzman, p. 55f.

return, is forced to write his own text, his interpretation of the case. Fiction becomes more real than 'reality'.

Writing, reading, and author(ity) are a constant preoccupation of the characters, authors, and narrators in the NYT. All characters involved in the quest for identity are writing texts themselves and are reading texts, that have or have not been written for them. Auster blends the ontologically distinct categories of author, character and narrator in classical detective fiction (and 'pre-postmodern' literature in general) on the one hand, and of reader, writer, detective and culprit on the other hand, and mixes different narrative situations in order to deconstruct them. He thus expands the relationships between these formerly distinct categories in narratology. Consequently, boundaries are blurred, and the text is robbed of its ultimate meaning, resembling a literature that Barthes has defined by its removal of the author.

> In precisely this way literature (it would be better from now on to say *writing*), by refusing to assign a 'secret', an ultimate meaning, to the text (and to the world as text), liberates what may be called an anti-theological activity, an activity that is truly revolutionary since to refuse to fix meaning is, in the end, to refuse God and his hypostases--reason, science, law.[277]

As Auster also includes himself in his work, he causes the novels to extend beyond their conventional bounds onto a metafictional level. The reader has to decode the narrative system but is doomed to fail, just like the detective, searching for the father-author-figure. Auster is not willing to present a single coherent narrative structure but rather offers multiple possibilities that are subject to interpretation and are dependent upon the reader's personal perspective. This strategy enables him to stress the complexity of the human subject, its constantly shifting nature, and the indeterminacy prevalent in today's world.

Language presents the biggest problem for the author, the characters and the readers of the NYT. Language is our most important medium of communication. Only language enables us to write a book, and only through language may we refer to objects in our world. Yet, in the NYT, language has proven to be arbitrary; language has lost its function as the element of order; language cannot convey ultimate meaning and fundamental truth; and language, expressed through words, fails in providing a solution to the cases, due to its inaccuracy. The question is, which of the

---

[277] Barthes, "The Death of the Author", p. 147.

following two perspectives of the relationship between the subject and language holds true: does language create the subject or does the subject create language? Unfortunately, the protagonists in the NYT have to surrender to the truth of the former, and cannot live with the fiction of the latter. In their attempt to define their self and the others' self through language, the characters must give in to the fact that language may never serve as an unambigiously comprehensible presence. Language is only able to represent reality but not to directly present it. The language of God, the prelapsarian speech in which a name was irrevocably attached to its object cannot be recreated. The fragmentation and plurality of the trilogy is created through the inaccuracy of the words that form the stories. Auster is aware of this and uses language as the main instrument to subvert and deconstruct the rationality and logic of the classical detective story.

In the NYT, Auster frequently refers to other literary works, mainly to American Romantic literature of the 19th century, but also to his own texts and to his own 'real' life. The literary references enable him to blend even more layers of texts into the novels, which further stresses the unclear distinction between fact and fiction. The multi-layered text itself turns into a case for the reader as he tries to make sense of Auster's allusions and 'literary mysteries'. An example of Auster's consistency in using these textual strategies is the "Wakefield" motif, which extends over all three stories. The same holds true for Auster's autobiographical references, which allow him to enter his own fiction. Cross-references between the stories support the intertextual character of the stories and hold the novels together. This is linked with the narrator's confession in TLR, that he is responsible for every story in the trilogy. Hence, these intertextual cross-references easily combine with the question of author(ity). The narrator in TLR combines beginning and end of the trilogy, as the "entire story comes down to what happened at the end, and without that end inside me now, I could not have started this book" (346). The problem is, however, that there is no such thing as a beginning or an end, which draws the trilogy further into "the circle of its repetition."

Auster's approach to the detective story is problematic to those readers who are accustomed to reading detective stories that operate under the conventions of classical or hard-boiled detective fiction. Of course, one of the things Auster wants to accomplish is to move away from established patterns and challenge his audience. Such is the mark of the mysteries that comprise *The New York Trilogy*, and such is the mark of the postmodern artist, as Spanos reminds us:

> The most immediate task (...) in which the contemporary writer must engage himself--it is, to borrow a phrase ungratefully from Yeats, the most difficult of tasks not impossible--is that of undermining the detectivelike expectations of the positivistic mind.[278]

Lyotard lends support to this argument in "Answering the Question: What is Postmodernism?":

> The postmodern would be that which (...) denies itself the solace of good forms, the consensus of a taste which would make it possible to share collectively the nostalgia for the unattainable; that which searches for new presentations, not in order to enjoy them but in order to impart a stronger sense of the unpresentable. A postmodern artist is in the position of a philosopher: the text he writes, the work he produces are not in principle governed by pre-established rules, and they cannot be judged according to a determining judgment, by applying familiar categories to a text or to the work. Those rules or categories are what the work of art itself is looking for. The artist and writer, then, are working without rules in order to formulate the rules of what *will have been done* [emphasis Lyotard's].[279]

With the NYT, Paul Auster has bridged the gap between postmodernism and the detective story. He skillfully combines the postmodern writer's natural inclination to 'misuse' common genres and literary conventions with the intention of expressing the inadequacies, the disorder and the existential void in our Western society with the pretension to writing detective fiction full of suspense, humor and irony. Auster "veers toward open, playful, optative, disjunctive, displaced, or indeterminate forms, a discourse of fragments, an ideology of fracture, a will to unmaking, an invocation of silences"[280] and yet succeeds in 'composing' a work of fiction that reads extremely well, is gripping and amusing.

This is possibly the main reason for Auster's growing commercial success in times when highly experimental, postmodern works are usually not among the best-selling books on the market. The NYT combines the familiar and successful features of the mystery and the detective novel with an ambitious and sophisticated style that lifts his books onto a higher literary level. He also touches a great variety of complex

---

[278] Spanos, p. 48.

[279] Jean-Francois Lyotard, "Answering the Question: What is Postmodernism?", in: Ihab and Sally Hassan (eds.), *Innovation/Renovation: New Perspectives on the Humanities* (Madison: University of Wisconsin Press, 1983), pp. 340/41.

[280] Hassan, "The Question of Postmodernism", p. 125.

social issues and problems that are so common in our postmodern society. The NYT is neither only plain and ordinary detective fiction, nor only postmodern literature, written for literary critics, experts and scholars. What is, however, probably the most important point, concerning Auster's popularity in Europe as well as in America and Asia, is his preoccupation with 'stories' and anecdotes, the creation of 'stories-within-stories'. This strategy enriches his novels and allows the reader to breathe, to lean back and enjoy a break from the complex issues of the deeper mysteries and from the hunt for 'postmodern clues'. Furthermore, they help the reader to understand the novels as such, since Auster frequently hides clues within these anecdotes. Is it not true, that "we all want to be told stories, and [that] we listen to them in the same way we did when we were young" (292)? In CoG, the character Auster asks Quinn after having explained his theory of Don Quixote, "to what extent people would tolerate blasphemies if they gave them amusement? The answer is obvious, isn't it? To any extent. For the proof is that we still read the book. It remains highly amusing to us. And that's finally all anyone wants out of a book--to be amused" (120). Auster's blasphemy may be to 'abuse' the classical detective novel for his metafictional experiments and his investigations of the nature, function and meaning of language. This, however, does not prevent his novels from attracting a large number of readers:

> Yet despite the death of the writer, the death of books, and the death of language, there seems to be one last reliable stable center in the confusion. Again and again the trilogy insists on the existence of the 'story', something we liked 'back in our childhood', stories Blue likes to spin, stories he likes to make up, stories the narrator finds in Fanshawe's letters, stories that do not necessarily make sense in a logical context but that are fun to read, like the story about Quinn in the dark apartment, where a tray of delicious food miraculously appears every day.[281]

Auster himself confirms this theory, when he says that "in the end, you don't only write the books you need to write, but write the books you would like to read yourself."[282] In the novels following the trilogy, Auster has kept up this concept. Similar events are repeated, characters we know from the NYT enter the scene once more, and allusions to other as well as his own works of fiction have ensured Auster's commercial success. One should, however, not forget, that he has created a unique, complex, yet still well-readable trilogy of detective stories, and thus a genre that I would finally like to define as "Austerian postmodern detective fiction." At the

---

[281] Freywald, p. 160-
[282] Auster, *The Art of Hunger*, p. 265.

intersection of postmodernism and detective fiction, Paul Auster has added some new dimensions to modern literature.

Bibliography

Ahrends, Günter. *Die amerikanische Kurzgeschichte: Theorie und Entwicklung.*
　　Stuttgart: Kohlhammer, 1980.

Alford, Steven E. "Mirrors of Madness: Paul Auster's *The New York Trilogy.*"
　　Critique 37:1, 1995: 17-33.

Alford, Steven E. "Spaced-Out: Signification and Space in Paul Auster's *The New*
　　York Trilogy." *Contemporary Literature* 36:4, 1995: 613-32.

Alsen, Eberhard. "Paul Auster's *Ghosts* and *Mr. Vertigo*: Homage to the Romantics."
　　Postmodern Studies 19: Romantic Postmodernism in American Fiction.
　　Amsterdam: Rodopi, 1996. 240-57.

Ashley, Kathleen and Leigh, Gilmore and Peters, Gerald. *Autobiography and*
　　Postmodernism. Amherst: University of Massachusetts Press, 1994.

Auster, Paul. *The Art of Hunger: Essays, Prefaces, Interviews.* Los Angeles: Sun and
　　Moon Press, 1992.

Auster, Paul. "The Decisive Moment." in: *The Art of Hunger.* Los Angeles: Sun and
　　Moon Press, 1992. 35-53.

Auster, Paul. *Hand to Mouth: A Chronicle of Early Failure.* New York: Henry Holt,
　　1997.

Auster, Paul. *The Invention of Solitude.* London: Faber and Faber, 1988.

Auster, Paul. *In the Country of Last Things.* London: Faber and Faber, 1987.

Auster, Paul. *Moon Palace.* New York: Penguin, 1989.

Auster, Paul. "New York Babel." in: *The Art of Hunger.* Los Angeles: Sun and Moon
　　Press, 1992. 26-34.

Auster, Paul. *The New York Trilogy.* New York: Penguin, 1990.

Auster, Paul. "Why Write?" *The New Yorker* 71:42, Dec. 1995 and Jan. 1996: 86-
　　89.

Barone, Dennis. "Auster's Memory." *The Review of Contemporary Fiction* 14:1,
　　1994: 32-34.

Barone, Dennis (ed.) *Beyond the Red Notebook: Essays on Paul Auster.* Philadelphia:
　　University of Pennsylvania Press, 1995.

Barone, Dennis (ed.) "Paul Auster/Danilo Kis Issue." *The Review of Contemporary Fiction* 14:1, 1994: 7-96.

Barth, John. "The Literature of Exhaustion." repr. in: *The Friday Book: Essays and Other Nonfiction*. New York: Putnam's Sons, 1984. 64-76.

Barth, John. *Lost in the Funhouse*. London: Secker and Warburg, 1969.

Barthes, Roland. "The Death of the Author." in: *Image-Music-Text*. London: Fontana, 1977. 142-48.

Barthes, Roland. *Roland Barthes par Roland Barthes*. Paris: Seuil, 1975.

Barthes, Roland. *S/Z*. trans. Richard Miller. New York: Hill, 1974.

Baudrillard, Jean. *America*. London: Verso, 1989.

Bawer, Bruce. "Doubles and More Doubles." *The New Criterion* 7:8, 1989: 67-74.

Baxter, Charles. "The Bureau of Missing Persons: Notes on Paul Auster's Fiction." *The Review of Contemporary Fiction* 14:1, 1994: 40-43.

Bennett, Donna. "The Detective Story: Towards a Definition of Genre." *PTL: A Journal for Descriptive Poetics and Theory of Literature* 4, 1979. 233-66.

Bernstein, Stephen. "Auster's Sublime Closure: *The Locked Room*." in: Barone, Dennis (ed.) *Beyond the Red Notebook: Essays on Paul Auster*. Philadelphia: University of Pennsylvania Press, 1995. 88-106.

Bertens, Hans. "The Detective." in: Bertens, Hans and Fokkema, Douwe (eds.) *International Postmodernism: Theory and Literary Practice*. Philadelphia: Benjamins, 1997. 195-202.

Bertens, Hans. *The Idea of the Postmodern: A History*. New York: Routledge, 1995.

Bertens, Hans. "The Postmodern *Weltanschauung* and its relation with Modernism: An Introductory Survey." in: Fokkema, Douwe and Bertens, Hans. *Approaching Postmodernism*. Philadelphia: Benjamins, 1986: 9-51.

Bertens, Hans and Fokkema, Douwe (eds.) *International Postmodernism: Theory and Literary Practice*. Philadelphia: Benjamins, 1997.

Bloom, Clive (ed.) *Twentieth-Century Suspense: The Thriller Comes of Age*. Houndmills: Macmillan Press, 1990.

Bloom, Clive and Docherty, Brian and Gibb, Jane and Shand, Keith. *Nineteenth-Century Suspense: From Poe to Conan Doyle*. Houndmills: Macmillan Press, 1988.

Bloom, Harold. *A Map of Misreading*.New York: Oxford University Press, 1975.

Bloom, Harold. *Poetry and Repression*. New Haven: Yale University Press, 1976.

Borges, Jorge Luis. *Ficciones*: *Obras Completas 1923-1972*. Buenos Aires: Emecé, 1974. 465-471.

Bradbury, Malcolm. *The Modern American Novel*. Oxford: Oxford University Press, 1992.

Brault, Pascale-Anne. "Translating the Impossible Debt: Paul Auster's *City of Glass*". *Critique* 39:3, 1998. 228-38.

Broich, Ulrich. "Intertextuality." in: Bertens, Hans and Fokkema, Douwe (eds.) *International Postmodernism: Theory and Literary Practice*. Philadelphia: Benjamins, 1997. 249-56.

Broich, Ulrich. "Ways of Marking Intertextuality." in: Bessière, Jean (ed.) *Fiction-Texte-Narratologie-Genre*. Proceedings of the 11th Congress of the International Comparative Literature Association. New York: Lang, 1989. 119-29.

Brooks, Peter. *Reading for the Plot: Design and Intention in Narrative*. New York: Knopf, 1984.

Bruckner, Pascal. "Paul Auster, or The Heir Intestate." in: Barone, Dennis (ed.) *Beyond the Red Notebook: Essays on Paul Auster*. Philadelphia: University of Pennsylvania Press, 1995. 27-33.

Buchloh, Paul G. and Becker, Jens P. *Der Detektivroman*. Darmstadt: Wissenschaftliche Buchgesellschaft, [3]1989.

Burkhardt, Rainer. *Die 'hartgesottene' amerikanische Detektivgeschichte und ihre gesellschaftliche Funktion* (Diss). Frankfurt a. M.: Peter Lang, 1978.

Cahoone, Lawrence (ed.) *From Modernism to Postmodernism: An Anthology*. Cambridge: Blackwell, 1996.

Carlson, Eric W. (ed.) *The Recognition of Edgar Allan Poe: Selected Criticism since 1829*. Ann Arbor: University of Michigan Press, 1966.

Cawelti, John G. *Adventure, Mystery, and Romance: Formula Stories as Art and Popular Culture*. Chicago: University of Chicago Press, 1976.

Chandler, Raymond. *Farewell, My Lovely*. Harmondsworth: Penguin, 1975.

Chandler, Raymond. "The Simple Art of Murder." in: Haycraft, Howard (ed.) *The Art of the Mystery Story*. New York: Biblo and Tannen, 1976. 228-47.

Chénetier, Marc. "Paul Auster's Pseudonymous World." in: Barone, Dennis (ed.) *Beyond the Red Notebook: Essays on Paul Auster*. Philadelphia: University of Pennsylvania Press, 1995. 34-43.

Contemporary Authors. New Revision Series, Vol 23. Straub, Deborah A (ed.) Detroit: Gale Research Company, 1988.

Creeley, Robert. "Austerities." *The Review of Contemporary Fiction* 14:1, 1994: 35-39.

Culler, Jonathan. *Dekonstruktion*: *Derrida und die poststrukturalistische Literaturtheorie*. Hamburg: Rowohlt, 1988.

Daube, David. *Die Geburt der Detektivgeschichte aus dem Geiste der Rhetorik*. Konstanz: Universitätsverlag, 1983.

Derrida, Jacques. *Positions*. trans. Alan Bass. Chicago: University of Chicago Press, 1978.

Derrida, Jacques. "Signature, Event, Context." in: *Limited Inc*. Evanston: Northwestern University Press, 1988. 1-23.

Derrida, Jacques. *Writing and Difference*. trans. Alan Bass. Chicago: University of Chicago Press, 1978.

Drenttel, William. "Paul Auster: A Selected Bibliography." in: Barone, Dennis (ed.) *Beyond the Red Notebook: Essays on Paul Auster*. Philadelphia: University of Pennsylvania Press, 1995. 189-98.

Dreyfus, Hubert L. and Rabinow, Paul. *Michel Foucault*: *Jenseits von Strukturalismus und Hermeneutik*. Weinheim: Athenäum, 1994.

Docherty, Brian (ed). *American Crime Fiction*: *Studies in the Genre*. Houndmills: Macmillan Press, 1988.

Dove, George N. *The Reader and the Detective Story*. Bowling Green: Bowling Green State University Press, 1996.

Ewert, Jeanne C. "Lost in the Hermeneutic Funhouse: Patrick Modiano's Postmodern Detective." in: Walker, Ronald et al. *The Cunning Craft: Original Essays on Detective Fiction and Contemporary Literary Theory*. Macomb: Western Illinois University Press, 1990: 166-73.

Federman, Raymond. "The Postmodern Artist." in: *Die Postmoderne--Ende der Avantgarde oder Neubeginn? Essays*. Eggingen: Edition Isele, 1989. 10-11.

Federman, Raymond. "Surfiction--Four Propositions in Form of an Introduction." in: Federman, Raymond (ed.) *Surfiction: Fiction Now...and Tomorrow*. Chicago: Swallow, 1981. 5-15.

Foucault, Michel. "Truth and Power." in: *Power/Knowledge*. trans. Colin Gordon. New York: Pantheon Books, 1980.

Freywald, Carin. "How Philip Marlowe Came to New York City: The Hard-Boiled American Crime Novel in Paul Auster's *The New York Trilogy*." Freese, Peter and Porsche, Michael (eds.) *Popular Culture in the United States: Proceedings of the German-American Conference in Paderborn, Sept. 14-17, 1993*. Essen: Die Blaue Eule, 1994. 143-60.

Fries, Udo. *The Structure of Texts*. (SPELL: Swiss Papers in English Language and Literature 3). Tübingen: Gunter Narr Verlag, 1987.

Gasser, Markus. *Die Postmoderne*. Stuttgart: M und P, 1997.

Gibson, Andrew. *Towards a Postmodern Theory of Narrative*. Edinburgh: Edinburgh University Press, 1996.

Goldstein, Rebecca. "The Man Shadowing Black is Blue." *New York Times Book Review*, June 29, 1986: 13.

Greenland, Colin. "The Novelist Vanishes." *Times Literary Supplement*, Dec. 11-17, 1987: 1375.

Gurganus, Allan. "How Do You Introduce Paul Auster in Three Minutes?" *The Review of Contemporary Fiction* 14:1, 1994: 7-12.

Handler, Nina. *Drawn into the Circle of its Repetition: Paul Auster's New York Trilogy*. San Bernardino: Borgo Press, 1996.

Hassan, Ihab. *The Dismemberment of Orpheus: Toward a Postmodern Literature*. Madison: University of Wisconsin Press, 1982.

Hassan, Ihab. *Paracriticisms: Seven Speculations of the Times*. Urbana: University of Illinois Press, 1975.

Hassan, Ihab. *The Postmodern Turn: Essays in Postmodern Theory and Culture*. Columbus: Ohio State University Press, 1987.

Hassan, Ihab. "Pluralism in Postmodern Perspective." *Critical Inquiry* 12, 1985/86: 503-20.

Hassan, Ihab. "POSTmodernISM: A Paracritical Bibliography". in: Lawrence Cahoone (ed.). *From Modernism to Postmodernism: An Anthology.* Cambridge: Blackwell, 1996. 382-400.

Hassan, Ihab. "The Question of Postmodernism." *Bucknell Review* 25:2, 1980: 117-26.

Hawthorne, Nathaniel. "Wakefield." in: *The Celestial Railroad and Other Stories.* New York: Penguin, 1980. 67-75.

Haycraft, Howard (ed.) *The Art of the Mystery Story.* New York: Biblo and Tannen, 1976.

Helmers, Hermann (ed.) *Verfremdung in der Literatur.* Darmstadt: Wissenschaftliche Buchgesellschaft, 1984.

Hilfer, Tony. *The Crime Novel: A Deviant Genre.* Austin: University of Texas Press, 1990.

Hindus, Milton (ed.) *Charles Reznikoff: Man and Poet.* Orono: The University of Maine at Orono University Press, 1984.

Holquist, Michael. "Whodunit and Other Questions: Metaphysical Detective Stories in Postwar Fiction." in: Most, Glenn W. and Stowe, William W (eds.) *The Poetics of Murder: Detective Fiction and Literary Theory.* San Diego: Harcourt, 1983. 156-73.

Holzapfel, Anne M. *The New York Trilogy: Whodunit?: Tracking the Structure of Paul Auster's Anti-Detective Novels.* Frankfurt a. M.: Peter Lang, 1996.

Hühn, Peter. "The Detective as Reader: Narrativity and Reading Concepts in Detective Fiction." *Modern Fiction Studies* 33:3, 1987: 451-66.

Hutcheon, Linda. *A Poetics of Postmodernism: History, Theory, Fiction.* New York: Routledge, 1988.

Huyssen, Andreas and Scherpe, Klaus R. (eds.) *Postmoderne: Zeichen eines kulturellen Wandels.* Hamburg: Rowohlt, [2]1993.

Irwin, John T. *The Mystery to a Solution: Poe, Borges, and the Analytic Detective Story.* Baltimore: John Hopkins University Press, 1994.

Irwin, Mark. "Memory's Escape: Inventing the *Music of Chance*--A Conversation with Paul Auster." *Denver Quarterly* 28:3, 1994: 111-22.

Jameson, Frederic. "Postmodernism and Consumer Society." in: Foster, Hal (ed.) *The Anti-Aesthetic: Essays on Postmodern Culture*. Seattle: Bay Press, 1983: 111-25.

Kendall, Joshua. "Psychische Zersplitterung in der postmodernen Polis: Kaspar Hauser in Paul Austers *The New York Trilogy*." in: Struve, Ulrich (ed.) *Der imaginierte Findling: Studien zur Kaspar-Hauser-Rezeption*. Heidelberg: Universitätsverlag, 1995. 207-22.

Kirkegaard, Peter. "Cities, Signs, and Meaning in Walter Benjamin and Paul Auster, or: never sure of any of it." *Orbis Litterarum* 48, 1993: 161-79.

Klepper, Martin. *Pynchon, Auster, DeLillo: Die amerikanische Postmoderne zwischen Spiel und Rekonstruktion*. Frankfurt a. M.: Campus Verlag, 1995.

Kreutzer, Eberhard. *New York in der zeitgenössischen amerikanischen Erzählliteratur*. Heidelberg: Carl Winter Universitätsverlag, 1985.

Kristeva, Julia. *Sèmeiotikè: Récherche pour une sémanalyse*. Paris: Seuil, 1969.

Lacan, Jacques. *Ecrits: A Selection*. New York: Norton, 1977.

Lacan, Jacques. "The Subject and the Other: Alienation." in: Miller, Jacques-Alain. *Four Fundamental Concepts*. New York: Norton, 1978.

Lavender, William. "The Novel of Critical Engagement: Paul Auster's *City of Glass*." *Contemporary Literature* 34:2, 1993: 219-39.

Leitch, Vincent B. *Postmodernism--Local Effects, Global Flows*. Albany: State University of New York Press, 1996.

Lewis, Barry. "The Strange Case of Paul Auster." *The Review of Contemporary Fiction* 14:1, 1994: 53-61.

Link, Franz H. *Edgar Allan Poe*. Frankfurt am Main: Athenäum, 1968.

Little, William G. "Nothing to Go On: Paul Auster's *City of Glass*." *Contemporary Literature* 38:1, 1997: 133-63.

Los Santos, Oscar de. "Auster vs. Chandler: Or, Cracking the Case of the Postmodern Mystery." *Connecticut Review* 16:1, 1994: 75-80.

Lyotard, Jean-Francois. "Answering the Question: What is Postmodernism?" in: Hassan, Ihab and Sally (eds.) *Innovation/Renovation: New Perspectives on the Humanities*. Madison: University of Wisconsin Press, 1983. 329-41.

Madsen, Deborah. *Postmodernism: A Bibliography, 1926-1994*. Amsterdam: Rodopi, 1995.

Malmgren, Carl D. "Detecting/Writing the Real: Paul Auster's *City of Glass*." in: D'haen, Theo and Bertens, Hans (eds.) *Narrative Turns and Minor Genres in Postmodernism*. Amsterdam: Rodopi, 1995. 177-201.

Margolies, Edward "The American Detective Thriller and the Idea of Society." in: Landrum, Larry N. and Browne, Pat and Browne, Ray B. (eds.) *Dimensions of Detective Fiction*. Bowling Green: Bowling Green University Popular Press, 1976. 71-89.

McHale, Brian. *Constructing Postmodernism*. New York: Routledge, 1992.

McHale, Brian. *Postmodernist Fiction*. New York: Methuen, 1987.

McPheron, William. "Remaking Narrative." *Poetics Journal* 7, 1987: 140-49.

Most, Glen W. and Stowe, William W. (eds.) *The Poetics of Murder: Detective Fiction and Literary Theory*. New York: Harcourt, 1983.

Nealon, Jeffrey T. "Work of the Detective, Work of the Writer: Paul Auster's *City of Glass*." *Modern Fiction Studies* 42:1, 1996: 91-110.

Neubauer, Paul. *Die Diskussion der US-amerikanischen Erzählliteratur der Postmoderne in der deutschsprachigen Amerikanistik*. Frankfurt a.M.: Peter Lang, 1994.

Nusser, Peter. *Der Kriminalroman*. Stuttgart: Metzler, 1980.

Olsen, Toby. "Metaphysical Mystery Tour." *New York Times Book Review*, Nov.3, 1985: 31.

Panek, LeRoy Lad. *An Introduction to the Detective Story*. Bowling Green: Bowling Green State University Popular Press, 1987.

Pfister, Manfred. "How Postmodern is Intertextuality?" in: Plett, Heinrich(ed.) *Intertextuality*.New York: De Gruyter, 1991. 207-24.

Poe, Edgar Allan. "The Murders in the Rue Morgue." in: *The Fall of the House of Usher and other Writings*. London: Penguin, 1986. 189-224.

Poe, Edgar Allan. "William Wilson." in: *The Fall of the House of Usher and Other Writings*. London: Penguin, 1986. 158-78.

Porter, Dennis. *The Pursuit of Crime*. New Haven: Yale University Press, 1981.

Priestman, Martin. *Crime Fiction: From Poe to the Present*. Plymouth: Northcote, 1998.

Pütz, Manfred. *The Story of Idenity: American Fiction of the Sixties*. München: Wilhelm Fink, [2]1987.

Pütz, Manfred and Freese, Peter (eds.) *Postmodernism in American Literature: A Critical Anthology*. Darmstadt: Thesen Verlag, 1984.

Rey, Santiago del. "Paul Auster: Metamorfosis del Misterio." *Quimera*, 90/91, 1989: 28-33.

Reyes, Alfonso. "About the Detective Novel." *The Literary Review* 38:1, 1994: 62-65.

Rosello, Mireille. "The Screener's Maps: Michel de Certeaus's 'Wandersmänner' and Paul Auster's Hypertextual Detective." in: George P. Landow (ed.) *Hyper/Text/Theory*. Baltimore: John Hopkins University Press, 1994. 121-58.

Rowen, Norma. "The Detective in Search of the Lost Tongue of Adam: Paul Auster's *City of Glass*." *Critique* 32:4, 1991: 224-34.

Russell, Alison. "Deconstructing *The New York Trilogy*: Paul Auster's Anti-Detective Fiction." *Critique* 31:2, 1990: 71-84.

Rutschky, Michael. "Die Erfindung der Einsamkeit: Der amerikanische Schriftsteller Paul Auster." *Merkur* 45:12, 1991: 1105-1113.

Saltzman, Arthur M. *Designs of Darkness in Contemporary American Fiction*. Philadelphia: University of Pennsylvania Press, 1990.

Sartre, Jean-Paul. *Existentialism*. Trans. Bernard Frechtman. New York: Philosophical Library, 1947.

Schiff, Stephen. "Inward Gaze of a Private Eye." *New York Times Book Review*, Jan. 4, 1987: 14.

Segal, Alex. "Secrecy and the Gift: Paul Auster's *The Locked Room*." *Critique* 39:3, 1998. 239-57.

Sorapure, Madeleine. "The Detective and the Author." in: Dennis Barone (ed.) *Beyond the Red Notebook*. Philadelphia: University of Pennsylvania Press, 1995. 71-87.

Spanos, William V. "The Detective and the Boundary: Some Notes on the Postmodern Literary Imagination." repr. in: *Repetitions: The Postmodern Occasion in Literature and Culture*. Baton Rouge: Louisiana State University Press, 1987. 13-49.

Sweeney, S.E. "Locked Rooms: Detective Fiction, Narrative Theory and Self-Reflexivity." in: Walker, Ronald et al. *The Cunning Craft: Original Essays on Detective Fiction and Contemporary Literary Theory*. Macomb: Western Illinois University Press, 1990: 1-14.

Symons, Julian. *Bloody Murder. From the Detective Story to the Crime Novel: A History*. New York: Viking Press, 1985.

Tani, Stefano. *The Doomed Detective: The Contribution of the Detective Novel to Postmodern American and Italian Fiction*. Carbondale: Southern Illinois University Press, 1984.

Todorov, Tzevtan. "The Typology of Detective Fiction." in: *The Poetics of Prose*. Ithaca: Cornell University Press, 1977. 42-52.

Tysh, Chris. "From One Mirror to Another: The Rhetoric of Disaffiliation in *City of Glass*." *The Review of Contemporary Fiction* 14:1, 1994: 46-52.

Van Dine, S.S. "Twenty Rules for Writing Detective Stories." in: Haycraft, Howard (ed.) *The Art of the Mystery Story*. New York: Biblo and Tannen, 1976. 189-193.

Versluys, Kristiaan (ed.) *Neo-Realism in Contemporary American Fiction*. Amsterdam: Rodopi, 1992.

Welsch, Wolfgang. *Unsere postmoderne Moderne*. Berlin: Akademie Verlag, [4]1994.

Wirth, Eric. "A Look back from the Horizon." in: Barone, Dennis (ed.) *Beyond the Red Notebook: Essays on Paul Auster*. Philadelphia: University of Pennsylvania Press, 1995. 171-82.

Zayed, Georges. *The Genius of Edgar Allan Poe*. Cambridge: Schenkman, 1985.

Ziegler, Heide (ed.) "The End of Postmodernism: New Directions." in: *Stuttgart Seminar in Cultural Studies*. Stuttgart: M und P Verlag, 1993. 5-10.

Diplomarbeiten Agentur

Die Diplomarbeiten Agentur vermarktet seit 1996 erfolgreich
Wirtschaftsstudien, Diplomarbeiten, Magisterarbeiten, Dissertationen
und andere Studienabschlußarbeiten aller Fachbereiche und Hochschulen.

Seriosität, Professionalität und Exklusivität prägen unsere Leistungen:

- Kostenlose Aufnahme der Arbeiten in unser Lieferprogramm

- Faire Beteiligung an den Verkaufserlösen

- Autorinnen und Autoren können den Verkaufspreis selber festlegen

- Effizientes Marketing über viele Distributionskanäle

- Präsenz im Internet unter **http://www.diplom.de**

- Umfangreiches Angebot von mehreren tausend Arbeiten

- Großer Bekanntheitsgrad durch Fernsehen, Hörfunk und Printmedien

Setzen Sie sich mit uns in Verbindung:

Diplomarbeiten Agentur
**Dipl. Kfm. Dipl. Hdl. Björn Bedey —
Dipl. Wi.-Ing. Martin Haschke ——
und Guido Meyer GbR ————**

**Hermannstal 119 k ————
22119 Hamburg ————**

**Fon: 040 / 655 99 20 ————
Fax: 040 / 655 99 222 ————**

**agentur@diplom.de ————
www.diplom.de ————**

Diplomarbeiten Agentur

www.diplom.de

- **Online-Katalog**
  mit mehreren tausend Studien

- **Online-Suchmaschine**
  für die individuelle Recherche

- **Online-Inhaltsangaben**
  zu jeder Studie kostenlos einsehbar

- **Online-Bestellfunktion**
  damit keine Zeit verloren geht

Wissensquellen gewinnbringend nutzen.

Wettbewerbsvorteile kostengünstig verschaffen.

Printed in Great Britain by
Amazon.co.uk, Ltd.,
Marston Gate.